Marta Cerezo Moreno, Nieves Pascual Soler (eds.)
Traces of Aging

Aging Studies | Volume 9

The series **Aging Studies** is edited by Heike Hartung, Ulla Kriebernegg and Roberta Maierhofer.

Marta Cerezo Moreno, Nieves Pascual Soler (eds.)
Traces of Aging
Old Age and Memory in Contemporary Narrative

[transcript]

We would like to thank the members of the research project *New Critical Approaches to the Trace and the Application to Recent Literature in English* (FFI2013-44154-P) and, in particular, its leading researcher Rosario Arias, for stimulating this research. We extend our sincere gratitude to Heike Hartung, Ulla Kriebernegg and Roberta Maierhofer for their enthusiasm for and commitment to this study. We express our thanks also to Ángeles de la Concha and Teresa Gibert for reading and commenting on early drafts of this book, and to Ellison Moorehead for the time taken to revise the text.

The publication of this volume has been supported by the University of Graz and the Spanish Ministry of Economy and Competitiveness.

This volume results from the collaboration of the Center for Inter-American Studies (University of Graz), the European Network in Aging Studies (ENAS) and the research project *New Critical Approaches to the Trace and the Application to Recent Literature in English* (FFI2013-44154-P).

Bibliographic information published by the Deutsche Nationalbibliothek
The Deutsche Nationalbibliothek lists this publication in the Deutsche Nationalbibliografie; detailed bibliographic data are available in the Internet at http://dnb.d-nb.de

© 2016 transcript Verlag, Bielefeld
All rights reserved. No part of this book may be reprinted or reproduced or utilized in any form or by any electronic, mechanical, or other means, now known or hereafter invented, including photocopying and recording, or in any information storage or retrieval system, without permission in writing from the publisher.

Cover layout: Kordula Röckenhaus, Bielefeld
Cover illustration: Carmen Pascual Soler, Almería, Spain, 2013.
Proofread by Ellison Moorehead
Printed in Germany
Print-ISBN 978-3-8376-3439-6
PDF-ISBN 978-3-8394-3439-0

Contents

Introduction
Literature that Returns to Life and the Mystique of Age
Marta Cerezo Moreno and Nieves Pascual Soler | 7

Keeping Appointments with the Past
Time, Place, and Narrative Identity in W.G. Sebald's *Austerlitz*
Anna MacDonald | 21

Haunted by a Traumatic Past
Age, Memory, and Narrative Identity in Margaret Atwood's
The Blind Assassin
Teresa Gibert | 41

"The whole aspect of age is full of possibilities!"
Traces of Ageing, Memory, and Sexuality in Daphne du Maurier's
"Don't Look Now"
Marta Miquel-Baldellou | 65

Ageing, Agency, and Autobiography
Challenging Ricoeur's Concept of Narrative Identity
Rahel Rivera Godoy-Benesch | 91

An Appetite for Life
Narrative, Time, and Identity in *Still Mine*
Pamela Gravagne | 111

**Memory, Dementia, and Narrative Identity in Alice Munro's
"The Bear Came Over the Mountain"**
Sara Strauss | 133

**Horror Mortis, Structural Trauma, and Postmodern Parody in
Saul Bellow's *Henderson the Rain King***
Francisco Collado-Rodríguez | 149

Rewriting the Story, Restorying the Self
Doris Lessing's Experiments in Life-Writing
Ángeles de la Concha | 169

Contributors | 189

Introduction

Literature that Returns to Life and the Mystique of Age

MARTA CEREZO MORENO AND NIEVES PASCUAL SOLER

> The effects of fiction, effects of revelation and transformation, are essentially effects of reading. It is by way of reading that literature returns to life, that is, to the practical and affective field of existence.
> (RICOEUR, *TIME AND NARRATIVE III* 101)

LITERATURE THAT RETURNS TO LIFE

Taking as its starting point the dialectic between Paul Ricoeur's concepts of the *trace* and *narrative identity* and based on the philosopher's belief that "fiction contributes to making life" ("Life in Quest of Narrative" 20) the present volume presents eight contributions that ponder the way narratives determine our understanding of human existence especially when configured at a late stage in life.[1] This articulation rests upon a disruption of

---

1 This volume results from the collaboration of the Center for Inter-American Studies (University of Graz), the European Network in Aging Studies (ENAS) and the research project *New Critical Approaches to the Trace and the Application to Recent Literature in English* (FFI2013-44154-P) financed by the Spanish Ministry of Economy and Competitiveness.

conceptualizing stages of life as "limited and static categories of understanding" (Cole xviii); that is, upon challenging what it means to grow old and experience time. Positioned within the discipline of Age/Ageing Studies, we aim to make insights into the reconceptualization of the concepts of living, ageing, death, creativity, continuity and change in accordance with Ricoeur's statement that the subject "appears both as a reader and the writer of its own life" (*Time and Narrative III* 246).

Ricoeur's philosophical views on subjectivity are based on his idea of the dynamic circularity connecting life and narrative. To the philosopher life and stories are both recounted and lived. He believes that the process of narrative composition is only completed by the reader since on the act of reading, of interpreting, – or what he calls refiguration or mimesis$_3$ – "rests the narrative's capacity to transfigure the experience of the reader" ("Life in Quest of Narrative" 26).[2] Reading is, thus, "a way of living in the fictive universe of the work" (27). To Ricoeur, the open world of the text intersects with the world of the reader creating what he calls a "horizon of experience" (26) that the reader appropriates in imagination. In this sense, stories are not just recounted, they are also lived. The intersection between life and narrative is reinforced by what Ricoeur calls the "pre-narrative structure of experience" or the conviction that experience has "a genuine demand for narrative" (29), since "life can be understood only by the stories that we tell about it" (31). Our lives are made of "story-fragments" from which a coherent narrative can be drawn out; such narrative can be "constitutive of [the subject's] *personal identity.*" Humans, then, can be said to be "tangled up in stories" that must be unravelled, that must be recounted and, as these stories emerge, "the implied subject also emerges" and narrative identity is constituted. Therefore, Ricoeur concludes, life is

---

2   In *Time and Narrative*, Ricoeur takes as his "guideline for exploring the mediation between time and narrative the articulation [...] between the three moments of mimesis that seriously and playfully, [he] named mimesis$_1$, mimesis$_2$, mimesis$_3$" (*Time and Narrative I* 53). Mimesis$_1$, also referred to as prefiguration, is defined as "a preunderstanding of the world of action, its meaningful structures, its symbolic resources, and its temporal character" (54). Mimesis$_2$ "opens up the world of the plot and institutes [...] the literariness of the work of literature" (53). Mimesis$_3$ "marks the intersection between the world of the text and the world of the listener or reader" (*Time and Narrative III* 159).

not just lived but also recounted and narrative fiction is consequently "an irreducible dimension of *self-understanding*" (30).

Ricoeur envisions narrative identity as constructed on the model of narrative plot with an internal dialectic of concordance and discordance that is given order and coherence by a process of emplotment.[3] The plot is therefore a dynamic structure, "an integrating process" which provides the story with a dynamic identity (21) by synthesizing and organizing the heterogeneous through configuration or mimesis$_2$, that is, by mediating between multiple incidents and a unified story and by drawing a durable temporal configuration out of a succession of passing events (22). In this conception of narrative Aristotle's notion of the "discordant concordance," – by which, for example, the discordant nature of *peripeteia* in tragedy is in clear dialogue with the ruling concordance of the plot – is central. Ricoeur observes the same dialectic between discordance and concordance in the construction of the narrative identity of a character which mediates between permanence and change, that is, between what could be considered a concordant and unified existence that follows the ordering nature of emplotment and discordant events that rupture that seeming unity. Narrative identity is unstable and changing and, in *Time and Narrative III*, is identified by Ricoeur with a category of identity which he calls *ipse* or selfhood, understood by the philosopher as a "dynamic identity" that "can include change, mutability, within the cohesion of one lifetime" (246) and that emerges by applying narrative configurations to the story of one's life and therefore by organizing it into a "coherent and acceptable story" (247). As a consequence, by telling, reading, and also listening to one's own experience self-knowledge is renewed. *Ipse* is in constant dialogue with what Ricoeur identifies as the other category of identity, *idem* or sameness, or a "subject identical with itself through the diversity of its different stages" – defined by the French philosopher as a "substantialist illusion" (246).

---

[3] "I have retained from Aristotle's *Poetics* the central concept of emplotment, which in Greek is *muthos* and which signifies both fable (in the sense of an imaginary story) and plot (in the sense of a well constructed story). It is this second aspect of Aristotle's *muthos* that I am taking as my guide" (Ricoeur, "Life in Quest of Narrative" 20-21).

The concept of the trace is essential in the construction of Ricoeur's narrative identity in narratives in which experience is revisioned by re-storying one's life and, therefore, by returning to the past. In *Time and Narrative III*, in his reflections on the relationship between the historic and narrative times, he introduces the concept of the trace. To the philosopher, history responds to the paradoxes of time phenomenology through historic time which mediates between the lived or personal experience of time and universal or cosmic time. Historic practice reinscribes time lived into cosmic time and reveals its creative capacity of time refiguration through connecting procedures that he calls *thought tools* like calendars, succession of generations, archives, documents, and, finally, traces. The source of authority of the document, Ricoeur argues, is the trace; the institutionalization of archives, the collection and conservation of documents are only possible because the past has left a mark. Therefore, to Ricoeur, history is "a knowledge by traces," which appeals "to the significance of a passed past that nevertheless remains preserved in its vestiges" (120). The trace is, consequently, "something present standing for something past" (183); it is a visible and permanent sign that denotes the presence of an absence or the presence of a passage, a term that signals the dynamics of a trace, as opposed to a mark, which implies static nature. The trace thus addresses us and "invites us to pursue it, to follow it back" (120).

In *Memory, History, and Forgetting* (2000), Ricoeur insists on the link of the trace to the past and oblivion, arguing that the destruction of traces results in an irreversible and definitive forgetfulness. The author argues that the reference to the past through traces is a paradox lodged in the origin of memory. The paradox would not exist if we only took into consideration the materiality of the presence of the trace. The dilemma arises because the trace is a mark of something which is absent, which has disappeared. "All memory is of the past" – as Aristotle points out in *Parva naturalia: On Memory and Recollection* – is, as Ricoeur states, the "loadstar for the rest of [his] exploration" (6). In his work, Ricoeur develops the Aristotelian distinction between *mnēmē*, "memory as appearing, ultimately passively, to the point of characterizing as an affection – pathos – the popping into mind of a memory" and *anamnēsis*, "the memory as an object of a search ordinarily named recall, recollection" (4). In the first case, the process of remembrance is passive, a simple evocation, that comes to our mind; the second consists of an active search. Both processes hold the aforementioned aporia: the presence of the absence through the trace of the past and its inscription in the human memory. Plato had already linked *anamnēsis* "to a prenatal knowledge from which we are said to have been separated by a forgetting that occurs when the life of the soul is infused into a body – described, moreover, as a tomb (*sōma-sēma*) – a forgetting from birth, which is held to make the search a relearning of what has been forgotten." Ricoeur designates recollection with the term *zētēsis*, which means searching; the rupture with the Platonic *anamnēsis* does not take place since *ana* means "returning to, retaking, recovering what had earlier been seen, experienced, or learned, hence signifies, in a sense, repetition." Forgetting "is thus designated obliquely as that against which the operation of recollection is directed" (27). Oblivion entails the destruction of traces, the definite absence of the past in the present. The active searching for memories shows one of the main goals of the act of remembrance: "struggling against forgetting, wresting a few scraps of memory from the 'rapacity' of time (Augustine dixit), from 'sinking' into oblivion" (30). It is a way "to coat with presence the otherness of that which is over and gone. In this memory is re-presentation, in the twofold sense of *re-:* turning back, anew" (39; emphasis added).

The contributions of this volume are mostly imbricated in a double process of both *anamnēsis* and *zētēsis*. First, they work on texts that develop in manifold ways the dialectic between concordance and discordance, change and permanence, absence and presence. This dialectic takes shape through the presentation of the inner functioning of memory processes, of recollection and forgetting, of the retracing of the past. This process entails the reconfiguration of their characters' sense of self and sense of the world they inhabit through the recovery of memory traces that trigger a re-reading and re-examination of their experiences and the constitution of their narrative identities. Second, the authors of this volume actively search for and delve into narrative traces imprinted in the works examined that invite them to *pursue them and follow them back*. The assay of these textual traces opens up different understandings of later stages of life and mostly dismantle old age as a *narrative of decline* (Gullette) or as the epitome of *narrative foreclosure* (Freeman, "Narrative Foreclosure") – that is, old age as a concluding chapter – and, therefore, point to the fact that later stages in life can also involve a continuous unfolding of personal growth. They exemplify Freeman's belief that old age is "the *narrative* phase par excellence" ("Death, Narrative Integrity" 394) from which existence, considered significantly by narrative gerontologists Randall and McKim as *texistence*, can be constantly re-evaluated and rewritten.

It is in the active reading or interpretation of the narratives proposed for analysis in this volume where we find, on the one hand, what Ricoeur calls "the decisive moment of narrative identity," and on the other hand, the space where "the notion of narrative identity encounters its limit and has to link up with the non narrative components in the formation of an acting subject" (*Time and Narrative III* 249). To Ricoeur, the reader exposes oneself to the text and "receive[s] a self enlarged by the appropriation of the proposed worlds that interpretation unfolds." Appropriation implies a "distantiation from oneself" or a "disappropiation of the self" that constitutes "the possibility of understanding oneself in front of the text" (*From Text to Action* 301). This entails a paradoxical situation in the process of self-constitution since narrative appropriation involves a certain degree of self-effacement and also an approach to the other through the identification with the fictional character; therefore, self-knowledge also implies learning about oneself from the other.

For Ricoeur, this space between the reader and the text, this cathartic encounter between the self and the other, is essentially ethical since narrative "is never ethically neutral, [and] proves to be the first *laboratory of moral judgment*" (*Oneself as Another* 140). Reading is "a moment of impetus" that moves the reader to self-knowledge but also to ethical action. By entering the various *horizons of experience* that the world of the text provides through the configuration of the other's narrative identity, the reader reads him/herself,[4] re-evaluates his/her inner and outer worlds and is invited to acknowledge his/her ethical responsibility: "Still it belongs to the reader, now an agent, an initiator of action, to choose among the multiple

---

4   "You know what importance I attach to the relation between text and reader. I always like to quote the beautiful text of Proust in *Time Regained*: 'But to return to myself, I thought more modestly of my book, and one could not exactly say that I thought of those who would read it, of my readers. Because they would not according to me be my readers, but the real readers of themselves, my book being only like one of those magnifying glasses offered to a customer by the optician at Combray. It was my book, and thanks to it I enabled them to read what lay within themselves'" (Ricoeur, "Narrative Identity" 198).

proposals of ethical justice brought forth by reading" (*Time and Narrative III* 249).

It is the purpose of this volume to present readings that intersect the world of the text with the world of the reader and that, through a process of refiguration of the narrative structures of that text, reveal the different horizons of experience that they encompass. The configurations of the eight narratives that are at stake are not ethically neutral and propose new ways of relating to the experience of growing old. We believe that the readings are in themselves initiations of action and change in relation to the culturally constructed views of later stages of the life course that socially displace individuals who are growing old. The readers' encounter with the ageing characters that inhabit the novels and film that are studied in the following pages is also an encounter with an other whose narrative identity helps the authors of the articles and us, their readers, to reflect on what human existence is about. In this sense, literature, as Ricoeur inspiringly states, returns to life.

THE MYSTIQUE OF AGE

In *Oneself as Another* Paul Ricoeur asserts that narratives have "a role to play in the apprenticeship of dying": they relieve our fear of "the unknown" (162). We should add that narratives also have a role to play in the apprenticeship of growing old: they relieve our fear of what we do not want to know, that is, the loss of others and our own death. In *The Fountain of Age* Betty Friedan refers to this denial of knowledge as the "age mystique" (33). Because old age is perceived as a problem we "never face the real problems that keep us from evolving" and alienate ourselves from "the actuality of our own experience" (62). Images of those "who can no longer 'pass' as young" are removed from memories and from sight. Segregated from society "in senior citizens' 'retirement homes' or nursing homes from which, like concentration camps, they will never return" (41), old people are denied, making age even more terrifying. Some contributors to this book offer alternatives to the mystique of age by looking at this stage of our lives as a transformation, a paradigm shift, a growth. Others examine narratives wherein the old feel cheated by life but determined to blockade fear. All of them confront the new realities of age through the particular narratives of individual old people ready to know.

In "Keeping Appointments with the Past: Time, Place, and Narrative Identity in W. G. Sebald's *Austerlitz*," Anna MacDonald investigates how physical places flood the imagination with images of the past through W. G. Sebald's final prose work, *Austerlitz* (2001). After Jacques Austerlitz, at the age of four and a half (in 1939), is forced to abandon Germany and emigrate to England, he represses all the memories that form his identity. Upon retiring from his teaching job at a London institute of art history, his defences break down and the repressed returns to his conscious mind. It is when he begins to remember that Austerlitz feels reborn, as if he had resurrected into life "almost on the eve of [his] death," (193) writes Sebald. This personal resurrection does not originate in the narcissistic desire to survive one's death but is born in accepting finitude and renouncing the consolation of eternity. And yet, the return, MacDonald argues, cannot be the ground for renewal lest memories are turned into words and life is reconfigured in narrative. So, in order to formulate his narrative identity and fill what MacDonald describes as "the void of missing, repressed or otherwise traumatizing personal as well as cultural memories," Austerlitz decides to travel to Prague, Terezín and Paris. In the Liverpool Street Station, the new Bibliothèque Nationale and the Antikos Bazar "individual and collective memories come together," reinforcing each other.

In *Memory, History, Forgetting* Ricoeur brings together architectural spaces "and that space unfolded by our corporeal condition" (150). Crucial to memory, he notes, is habitation: "the memory of having inhabited some house in some town or some part of the world are particularly eloquent and telling" (148). While the protagonist of Sebald's text travels to a world he does not know, Iris Chase, the eighty-two year old narrator of Margaret Atwood's *The Blind Assassin*, revisits Avilion, her grandmother Adelia's Victorian mansion where she grew, to remember what has been forgotten. Teresa Gibert in "Haunted by a Traumatic Past: Age, Memory and Narrative Identity in Margaret Atwood's *The Blind Assassin*" studies the places of memory in Atwood's Booker Prize-winning novel (published when the author was sixty-one) within the conceptual framework of Ricoeur's theory of habitation. Perceptively, among these places she includes the text of the romance entitled "The Blind Assassin" itself, "a literary memorial," as Gibert describes it in honour of Iris's sister, Laura, that keeps her remembrance alive and available, and "an act of atonement" for the offences of her remembered selves.

Also delving into sensual memory and literature as atonement is the essay "'The whole aspect of age is full of possibilities!': Traces of Ageing, Memory, and Sexuality in Daphne du Maurier's 'Don't Look Now'" by Marta Miquel-Baldellou. It is to Venice, though, where Daphne du Maurier travels so as to come to terms with the deaths of her close friend Gertrude Lawrence and her husband Frederick Browning. As a result she writes "Don't Look Now," a short story where a couple goes on a trip to the Reppublica Serenissima to forget the demise of their young daughter. There they encounter two old dwarf twins who force the couple to face their suffering. Miquel-Baldellou argues that "the twins become ageing doubles of the protagonists of the story" and, significantly, replicate "the death of the author's literary persona." Miquel-Baldellou examines du Maurier's obsession with the decline of old age and the way it impacted her writing using Ricoeur's theories on narrative identity, imagination, and time. Throughout the development of her argument, she raises two other issues. One relates to the gothic mode in which the experience of loss is conveyed. Concerned as it is with death and the dissolution of identity, the gothic – she sustains – jeopardises the will to forget the past that dominates these parents. The other concerns the literary connotations of decay attached to the city of Venice and how its maze of labyrinthine streets circulate, haunt and move characters and author to emotional turmoil.

The limits of Ricoeur's concept of narrative identity are probed by Rahel Rivera Godoy-Benesch in "Ageing, Agency, and Autobiography: Challenging Ricoeur's Concept of Narrative Identity." In Ricoeur's view, the assertion of identity in narrative relies on personal agency, the exercise of which depends on what Rivera Godoy-Benesch calls "a functioning mind" and the continuity of memory. Old age, however, is characterised by physical decline across all sensory systems which in turn causes a decrease of mind activity and, ultimately, of agency. Drawing on Stephen G. Post, who denounces the value of promoting reason at the cost of emotions in our society, the author calls for a new kind of narrative identity based not on "the agency of the mind" but on the capacity to feel and the sensual nature of memory. Through this lens she reads two short stories by John Barth ("Peeing Tom" and "Assisted Living," collected in *The Development*,

2008) and Joan Didion's autobiographies *The Year of Magical Thinking* (2005) and *Blue Nights* (2011).

It is the discontinuity of memory and the continuity of narrative that concerns Pamela Gravagne in "An Appetite for Life: Narrative, Time, and Identity in *Still Mine*," but her treatment of the topic differs from Godoy-Benesch's. In the film *Still Mine* (2013), directed by Michael McGowan, an old man fights against local authorities in rural New Brunswick to build a new home for his wife, affected by dementia, and himself because the house they live in no longer meets their needs. Through Craig Morrison's determination to continue building in spite of official regulations, Gravagne illustrates Ricoeur's determination to honour life by living up to death with what Olivier Abel calls "the grace of insouciance" (xiii). The posthumously published *Living Up to Death*, a collection of sketches written by Ricoeur in the last years of his life, supports the claim that his "insouciance" for life involves both the agony of effacing oneself or the suffering of self-detachment and the cheerfulness of letting go of oneself. His conception reflects the influences of Spinoza's faith on remaining alive to the end, Aristotle's anthropology of human vulnerability and Kant's obsession with an afterlife. Using these hermeneutic tools Gravagne shows that by building a home Craig builds a life message that, she writes, "enriches and enlarges, rather than diminishes, our idea of self and story as we grow older."

The theme of dementia is tackled by Sara Strauss in "Memory, Dementia and Narrative Identity in Alice Munro's 'The Bear Came Over the Mountain.'" In this short story the Nobel Prize-winning Canadian author narrates the development of Alzheimer's disease in Fiona and her husband's fight with the sickness. In Strauss's words, the article shows "how Munro's narrative, which is told from Grant's point of view, deals with the all-embracing effects of memory loss on the patients' and their relatives' lives and illustrates the relatives' struggle to comprehend the changes of identity dementia entails." Following upon the ethical functions of narratives theorised by Ricoeur in *Time and Narrative III* and his view of identity as a structure of self-constancy that nevertheless includes change, Strauß concludes by reflecting on the need of readers to empathise with the plight of others so as to reconfigure our identity and change behaviours.

For his part, Francisco Collado-Rodríguez looks into the narrativity of death in "Horror Mortis, Structural Trauma, and Postmodern Parody in Saul Bellow's *Henderson the Rain King*" but from a different perspective than

Ricoeur. He analyses Eugene Henderson's trauma of death at the core of his old age using Sigmund Freud's account of dream-interpretation and Joseph Campbell's myth archetypes. Collado-Rodríguez concludes that Bellow manipulates the traces of the past by parodying modernist symbols and that it is through this ridiculous imitation that the American writer transcends the logic of narrative closure. It is perhaps appropriate, given the intent of this volume, to read the alternative focus underlying this essay in light of Ricoeur's philosophy of the symbol to which he turns his attention in *The Symbolism of Evil*. At the end of the book the French philosopher sums up his task thus:

> The task of the philosopher, guided by symbols would be to break out of the enchanted closure of consciousness of oneself, to end the prerogative of self-reflection [...] symbols [and] myths [...] speak of the situation of man in the being of the world. The task, then, is starting from the symbols, to elaborate existential concepts – that is to say, not only structures of reflection but structures of existence – insofar as existence is the being of man. (356-57)

Henderson was unable to develop the existential concepts he needed to face the birth of death. Not so Bellow who, in the words of Collado-Rodríguez, forces "in his readers ideological reflections on [the] present" which help organise the postmodern structure of existence in an intelligible manner.

This volume ends with an essay on autobiography and the narration of one's life into old age. Ángeles de la Concha explores Doris Lessing's impulse to tell her story in her novels, from the pentalogy *Children of Violence* which saw the light in 1952 to *The Sweetest Dream*, published in 2001, when she turned eighty-three. As to the choice of fiction to explain Lessing's experiments in life-writing, de la Concha sides with Ricoeur when he claims that, "It is precisely because of the elusive character of real life that we need the help of fiction to organise life retrospectively, after the fact, prepared to take as provisional and open to revision any figure of emplotment borrowed from fiction or from history" (*Oneself as Another* 162). In this understanding, she argues that for Lessing old age is a privileged position from which to organise her identity, rework unsolved matters, heal the wounds open since childhood and, in sum, live the "good life" she dreamed of.

Contributors to this book deal with the dialectics of ageing and agency, concordance and discordance, narrative and life, time and space, trace and erasure, memory and oblivion, continuity and discontinuity. They base their studies on the theories of Paul Ricoeur, which are used to explain differences across life experiences and similarities in narrative structures. Through the various traces of aging that the authors of this volume discover in the stories of old age that they tell, it aims to help untangling the dynamic identities that can be hold in later stages of life.

REFERENCES

Abel, Olivier. Preface. *Living Up to Death.* By Paul Ricoeur. Chicago: U of Chicago P, 2009. vii-xxii. Print.

Cole, Thomas R. *The Journey of Life: A Cultural History of Aging in America.* Cambridge: Cambridge UP, 1992. Print.

Freeman, Mark P. "Narrative Foreclosure in Later Life: Possibilities and Limits." *Storying Later Life. Issues, Investigations, and Interventions in Narrative Gerontology.* Ed. Gary Kenyon, Ernst Bohlmeijer, and William L. Randall. Oxford: Oxford UP, 2011. 3-19. Print.

---. "Death, Narrative Integrity, and the Radical Challenge of Self-understanding: A Reading of Tolstoy's *Death of Ivan Ilych.*" *Ageing and Society* 17 (1997): 373-98. Print.

Friedan, Betty. *The Fountain of Age.* New York: Simon & Schuster, 1993. Print.

Gullette, Margaret Morganroth. *Declining to Decline: Cultural Combat and the Politics of the Midlife.* Charlottesville: UP of Virginia, 1997. Print.

Post, Stephen G. "*Respectare*: Moral Respect for the Lives of the Deeply Forgetful." *Dementia: Mind, Meaning, and the Person.* Ed. Julian C. Hughes, Stephen C. Louw, and Steven R. Sabat. Oxford: Oxford UP, 2006. 223–34. Print.

Randall, William L. and A. Elizabeth McKim. "Reading Life: The Interpreting of Texistence." *Reading Our Lives. The Poetics of Growing Old.* Oxford: Oxford UP, 2008. 95-113. Print.

Ricoeur, Paul. *Living Up to Death.* Trans. David Pellauer. Chicago: U of Chicago P, 2009. Print.

---. *Memory, History, Forgetting*. Trans. Kathleen Blamey and David Pellauer. Chicago: U of Chicago P, 2006. Print.
---. *Oneself as Another*. Trans. Kathleen Blamey. Chicago: U of Chicago P, 1994. Print.
---. *From Text to Action. Essays in Hermeneutics, II*. Trans. Kathleen Blamey and John B. Thompson. Evanston: Northwestern UP, 1991. Print.
---. "Life in Quest of Narrative." *On Paul Ricoeur. Narrative and Interpretation*. Ed. David Wood. London: Routledge, 1991. 20-33. Print.
---. "Narrative Identity." *On Paul Ricoeur. Narrative and Interpretation.* Ed. David Wood. London: Routledge, 1991. 188-99. Print.
---. *Time and Narrative*. Vol. 1. Trans. Kathleen Blamey and David Pellauer. Chicago: U of Chicago P, 1990. Print.
---. *Time and Narrative*. Vol. 3. Trans. Kathleen Blamey and David Pellauer. Chicago: U of Chicago P, 1990. Print.
---. *The Symbolism of Evil*. Trans. E. Buchanan. Boston: Beacon Press, 1967. Print.
Sebald, Winfried Georg. *Austerlitz*. Trans. Anthea Bell. Harmondsworth: Penguin, 2001. Print.

Keeping Appointments with the Past
Time, Place, and Narrative Identity in
W.G. Sebald's *Austerlitz*

ANNA MACDONALD

W. G. Sebald's final prose work, *Austerlitz* (2001), is a disquisition on the nature of time and the intimate relationship between material traces of the past, memory, and narrative identity. In this book, Sebald proposes what the narrator describes as "a kind of historical metaphysic, bringing remembered events back to life" (14). Importantly, these remembered events, traces of which persist in the present and extend into the future, are all encountered in place.

In 1939, at the age of four and a half, Jacques Austerlitz was forced to emigrate to England as part of the *Kindertransport* that evacuated children from German-occupied territories before the outbreak of war. For sixty years, he repressed the memories of his exile, his origins and identity. But at the onset of old age, as he describes it to the book's narrator "almost on the eve of my death" (193), Austerlitz's defences begin to break down. "It was," he says, "as if an illness that had been latent in me for a long time were now threatening to erupt, as if some soul-destroying and inexorable force had fastened upon me and would gradually paralyse my entire system" (173-74). Before he can begin to know his identity, and certainly before he can find a cogent way of narrating it, Austerlitz's existing sense of self (fragile as it is) must be "destroyed."

Having retired from his position as a lecturer at a London institute of art history, Austerlitz planned to collate the extensive materials he had collected throughout his working life into a book investigating the "history of architecture and civilization" (170). Instead, in the absence of his teaching and research routines, he experiences the first of a series of mental breakdowns and the "disintegration of [his] personality" (174). "I sensed," Austerlitz tells the narrator, "that in truth I had neither memory nor power of thought, nor even any existence, that all my life had been a constant process of obliteration, a turning away from myself and the world" (174).

It is only after the eruption of the "illness latent" within him that Austerlitz can begin to piece together his history via the often painful access of formerly repressed memories which are triggered by encounters with material traces of the past. Austerlitz travels into memory in search of his identity, his origins and history, the retrospective relation of which composes the bulk of the text. These travels take the form of actual journeys to the witnessing sites of his childhood experiences where, he considers, he has "appointments to keep" with the past (360).

In this chapter, I will examine some of the most critical of these witnessing sites of memory at which Austerlitz has appointments to keep: London's Liverpool Street Station, Prague, Terezín, and Paris. Austerlitz's journey into memory via places such as these, and the attempts he then makes to discover the "proper order" (61) in which to tell his story to the narrator, also enquires into the ways in which material traces of the past, encountered *in situ*, prompt the emergence of formerly repressed memories and bring past events back to life. It is these *living* connections with the past that Austerlitz travels to find.

Numerous scholars have emphasised the importance of travel in Sebald's prose. Massimo Leone has argued that in Sebald's work "the exploration of space replaces an impossible exploration of time and memory" (100). Karin Bauer contends that "Austerlitz and his fictional biographer [...] are largely defined by and preoccupied with movement through space and time." In the case of Austerlitz, she considers this movement to be motivated by a "search for his own ever-elusive history and identity" (235). For many scholars, the transitory nature of Sebald's characters, including Austerlitz, stems from and ultimately reflects the traumatic experience of exile from the homeland and from the self. One of the most common (although not uncontested) readings of *Austerlitz* is as a trauma narrative. Katya Garloff considers that "Sebald's writings resonate with the contemporary discourse of trauma in psychoanalysis, philosophy, and literary criticism." She argues that *Austerlitz* "incorporates the logic of trauma into the very form of the text" (158). By way of example, Garloff considers the "chance encounters" between Austerlitz and the narrator, which frame the narrative, to be "equivalents of the flashbacks and other manifestations of *mémoire involuntaire* through which Austerlitz gains access to his repressed memories" (161).

Even more important than his encounters with the narrator, however, are Austerlitz's encounters with the material traces of his past in place. J.J. Long suggests as much when he makes the case for a Proustian reading of Austerlitz's return to Prague (discussed in detail below) according to which

> the implication of *mémoire involuntaire* is that somatosensory memory [as it occurs in place] is both more powerful and more authentic than voluntary memory [...] The crooked paving stones of Prague emphasise the privileged status of moments of sensory [...] recall that bypass conscious mental efforts at recollection. (157)

As such, it is via material traces of the past that "bypass conscious mental efforts" which for Austerlitz have been employed in *avoiding* recollection and *defending* himself against the return of the repressed, that memory is allowed once more to emerge.

But the emergence of Austerlitz's memory and identity have as much to do with *reliving* past events as they do with purely "mental efforts of recollection." In keeping with his emphasis upon remembering in place and his "historical metaphysic," which looks forward to "bringing remembered events back to life," Austerlitz's conception of time has a spatial quality and a *volume* that I will return to throughout this essay. He describes the notion of time thus:

> I have always resisted the power of time out of some internal compulsion which I myself have never understood, keeping myself apart from so-called current events in the hope, as I now think, [...] that time will not pass away, has not passed away, that I can turn back and go behind it, and there I shall find everything as it once was, or more precisely I shall find that all moments of time have co-existed simultaneously, in which case none of what history tells us would be true, past events have not occurred but are waiting to do so at the moment when we think of them [...]. (144)

In time, in the return of memories as they are encountered in place, Austerlitz looks for the consistency and continuity which has been denied to him as a result of the loss of his origins, his memories of childhood, and his identity. If time "has not passed away," if "all moments of time have co-existed simultaneously" and we can, as a result, "turn back and go behind" time and experience past events "at the moment when we think of them," then Austerlitz's memory and identity, despite being repressed for almost sixty years, are not in fact lost. For all the painful effort he has expended in "keeping [himself] apart," if he travels in the right way, turning back and going behind, Austerlitz should (in theory) be able to access a narrative identity that was interrupted at the age of four and a half at the moment of his forced exile but which nevertheless has remained unchanged throughout his lifetime.

Austerlitz's journey can be read as a search for "places which have more of the past about them than the present" (259) and certainly Liverpool Street Station, Prague, Terezín, and Paris are examples of these. There is, nevertheless, a sense in which all of these situated traces of the past are under threat. This threat finds its way into the recomposition of Austerlitz's narrative identity and is experienced as "a sense of disjunction, of having no ground beneath my feet" (154). But these continuing (one might, of Austerlitz's identity, even describe them as *constitutive*) anxieties do not prevent him from working to "go behind time" and keep his "appointments in the past."

Thinking of the past, for Austerlitz, always happens in place, at witnessing sites of memory, sparked by the material traces of past events that, borrowing from Paul Ricoeur, have been left behind (Ricoeur, *Time and Narrative III* 119). Austerlitz's travels across Europe are in effect an enactment of the exhortation of the trace which according to Ricoeur "invites us to pursue it, to follow it back, if possible, to the person … who has passed this way" (120). Indeed, Austerlitz's story is an apt reflection of the (rhetorical) questions that shape Ricoeur's meditation on the trace, memory, and the three-fold present: "Is not the trace, as trace, present? Is to follow it not to render contemporary with their trace the events that it leads back to? […] In short, is the past intelligible in any other way than as persisting in the present?" (144).

Axel Goodbody, drawing on the work of Aleida Assmann, has identified "texts, images, the body and places as the four principal media through which memories and identity are anchored in cultural memory" (59-60). In his elaboration of the intimate relationship between place and cultural memory, Goodbody adopts Assmann's argument to stress the ways in which "lingering material traces [...] constitute physical links mediating between present and past" (60). Goodbody's approach to sites of memory has much to offer a reading of *Austerlitz* that emphasises his encounters of material traces of the past in place as a means of accessing memories and formulating a narrative identity. According to Goodbody's analysis,

> places of memory [are] auratic sites of immediate encounter with a forgotten past. Places are special symbols of events and associated values because they possess an indexical relationship with meaning. Not only do they bridge the gap between mental constructs and reality with a unique degree of physical validity and longevity, they are also typically sites where individual and collective memories reinforce each other. (60)

The places to which Austerlitz returns in order to "go behind" time and experience past events are all, always, sites where individual and collective memories come together and "reinforce each other."

In order to enforce the "avoidance system" (Sebald 278) which has for the best part of his life allowed Austerlitz to work against the resurfacing of traumatic memories, he also refuses to engage with historical events and cultural memories that extend beyond the nineteenth century. Austerlitz tells the narrator:

> Inconceivably as it seems to me today, I knew nothing about the conquest of Europe by the Germans and the slave state they set up, and nothing about the persecution I had escaped [...] As far as I was concerned the world ended in the late nineteenth century. I dared go no further than that [...] I did not read newspapers because, as I now know, I feared unwelcome revelations, I turned on the radio only at certain hours of the day, I was always refining my defensive reactions, creating a kind of quarantine or immune system which, as I maintained my existence in a smaller and smaller space, protected me from anything that could be connected in any way, however distant, with my own history. (197-98)

Austerlitz cannot "quarantine" himself from his own history, which is to say his memory and identity, without also "defending" himself from twentieth century history and the collective memories that belong to it. Consequently, as will become apparent in what follows, the gradual emergence of those individual memories he has worked so hard to keep at bay is also the emergence of the cultural memories of "the persecution [he] had escaped." These individual and collective memories are triggered by the encounter of the same material traces of the past at the same sites: Liverpool Street Station, Prague, Terezín, and Paris.

At retirement age, faced with the "disintegration of [his] personality," the oppressive absence of memory and identity "and to escape the insomnia which increasingly tormented me" (178), Austerlitz takes to wandering the streets of Greater London at night. On these nocturnal peregrinations, he is "always irresistibly drawn back" to Liverpool Street Station (180), to which (unbeknownst to him at that time) *Kindertransport* trains had arrived from mainland Europe in 1939. Liverpool Street is the station on Austerlitz's journey that marks his entry into England and the subsequent loss of his name, memory, and identity. It is one of those witnessing sites of memory that, for Austerlitz and for the composition of his narrative identity, captures "'here' (in space) and 'now' (in the present), the past passage of living beings" (Ricoeur, *Time and Narrative III* 120). And it is "here" and "now" that the first stirrings of Austerlitz's long-repressed memories, the first glimmer of his origins and identity, begin to surface.

To the narrator, Austerlitz describes the emergence of memory at Liverpool Street thus:

the crucial point was […] the scraps of memory beginning to drift through the outlying regions of my mind […] memories behind and within which many things much further back in the past seemed to live, all interlocking like the labyrinthine vaults I saw in the dusty grey light, and which seemed to go on forever. In fact I felt, […] that the waiting-room where I stood as if dazzled contained all the hours of my past life, all the suppressed and extinguished fears and wishes I had ever entertained, as if the black and white diamond pattern of the stone slabs beneath my feet were the board on which the endgame would be played, and it covered the entire plane of time. (191-93)

Liverpool Street Station is one of those witnessing sites of memory at which it seems, to Austerlitz, possible to "turn back and go behind time" (144). It is here, at his entrance to England as a small boy, and now, "almost on the eve of [his] death" (193), that the door accessing the spaces of Austerlitz's memory is unlocked. Liverpool Street is the first of those places in *Austerlitz* that suggest a conception of time that emphasises *continuity*, a place in which "all moments [...] co-existed simultaneously" (144), which "contained all the hours of my past life"; "labyrinthine vaults" that reveal "memories behind and within which many things much further back in the past seemed to live."

Liverpool Street is a trigger for the resurgence of Austerlitz's long-repressed memories and a crucial example of the ways in which spatial traces function in the delayed composition of his narrative identity. This episode also captures Sebald's use of the concept of the trace to explore the notion of time, according to his (which is also Austerlitz's) "historical metaphysic."

Ricoeur has emphasised the importance of place and space to our understanding of memory and the location, so to speak, of the past and the future. In the first volume of *Time and Narrative*, and following Augustine, he asks:

Is it because the question has been posed in terms of "place" (*where* are future and past things?) that we obtain a reply in terms of "place" (*in* the soul, *in* the memory)? Or is it not instead the quasi-spatiality of the impression-image and the sign-image inscribed in the soul, that calls for the question of the location of the future and past things? (Ricoeur, *Time and Narrative I* 12)

For Sebald, and for Austerlitz, time – past, present and future – is always *located*. Austerlitz conceives of memory as an architectural space, much like Liverpool Street Station, of "interlocking [...] labyrinthine vaults." This notion of labyrinthine, interlocking spaces is one that he repeatedly returns to in his narrative as in the journeys that he makes. In Prague, for instance, where he travels in search of his origins, Austerlitz feels, as he did at Liverpool Street, "as if the dead were returning from their exile and filling the twilight around me with their strangely slow but incessant to-ing and fro-ing" (188). The dead, for Austerlitz, come to life in the spaces of memory through the material traces they have left behind. This movement of the dead among the living, which is indicative of the persistence of the past in the present, has a radical effect on his understanding of the nature of time. In Prague, where as I will discuss below Austerlitz again finds his memories located, and returning via material traces of the past, he concludes that, "It does not seem to me [...] that we understand the laws governing the return of the past, [...] I feel more and more as if time did not exist at all, only various spaces interlocking according to the rules of a higher form of stereometry, between which the living and the dead can move back and forth as they like" (261).

The notion which Austerlitz stresses of being able to go "behind" the surface and to discover "things much further back in the past" is one to which he returns throughout his narrative. This spatial conception is important for a number of reasons. It emphasises a *depth* of time, memory, and narrative. It permits movement between the surface and what lies beneath it (for Sebald, as for Austerlitz, this movement is always characterised by the passage between the living and the dead who come to *life* in places that "have more of the past about them than the present" [259]). It complicates the notion of a one-dimensional "plane of time" and instead gives credence (and *volume*) to Ricoeur's three-fold present, "the present of the future, the present of the past, and the present of the present" (Ricoeur, *Time and Narrative I* 21). And it defines a *space* for time, populated by the material traces of what has passed but which, through the persistence of such traces, 'has not passed away' (Sebald 144; emphasis added).

Austerlitz's desire to move "behind" his memories, to find there "all the hours of my [...] life" which have passed but which have "not passed away," allows the reader to make sense of his travels in search of material traces of the past in the present and the composition of his narrative identity "in transit" (Ricoeur, *Time and Narrative I* 13).

The first encounter with material traces of the past and his experience of the return of the dead at Liverpool Street Station triggers vivid dreams in which, "somewhere behind his eyes, [Austerlitz explains, he] had felt [...] overwhelmingly immediate images forcing their way out of him" (197). These dreams and the circumstances leading up to them compel Austerlitz to acknowledge "how little practice I had in using my memory, and conversely how hard I must always have tried to recollect as little as possible, avoiding everything which related in any way to my unknown past" (197). This marks a critical juncture in the text in which Austerlitz reflects upon the active (if unconscious) role he has played in the continued suppression of painful memories and the ways in which he has attempted to fill the void left behind by his refusal of narrative identity with research into pre-twentieth century architecture and civilization. Austerlitz comes to understand that his research "served as a substitute or compensatory memory" (198). It is unsurprising that this "compensatory memory" and with it Austerlitz's provisional identity, breaks down at the age of his retirement, a breakdown that leads to his nocturnal peregrinations, the involuntary emergence of early memories at Liverpool Street and eventually the decision to travel to Prague in search of his origins and identity.

Like J.J. Long, Karin Bauer has emphasised the sensual nature of Austerlitz's travels into memory. Of his encounter with the past at Liverpool Street Station, she argues,

it is not merely the physical existence of the cultural artifact or architectural monument that inevitably attests to the presence of the past; rather, it is the presence of the past experienced in the now that constitutes our connection to it. This experience of the past is, however, not an intellectual experience of the historian who accumulates knowledge about the past; rather it is a sensual, ephemeral event – the 'cold breath of air' – occasioned by the physical manifestations of the past that serves as a trigger for the experience of sensations and images. (245)

In Bauer's formulation of the sensual encounter with the past we find an echo of Ricoeur's concept of the trace. Liverpool Street Station is one such "site of Austerlitz's [sensual] encounter with his own past" (Bauer 245) and marks the beginning of his "investigation" into his "own history" (Sebald 95).

The streets of Prague are another. Returning to the city from which he was exiled at the age of four and a half, Austerlitz visits the state archives to obtain a list of people bearing his name who were living there between 1934 and 1939. As a result of this research, as Austerlitz relates to the narrator,

no sooner had I arrived in Prague than I found myself back among the scenes of my early childhood, every trace of which had been expunged from my memory for as long as I could recollect. As I walked through the labyrinth of alleyways, thoroughfares and courtyards [...], and still more so when I felt the uneven paving [...] underfoot [...], it was as if I had already been this way before and memories were revealing themselves to me not by means of any mental effort but through my senses, so long numbed and now coming back to life. (212-13)

This episode is a critical example of Austerlitz's "historical metaphysic," the return to life of details of the past which have lingered in material traces. In Austerlitz's return to Prague, we find certain characteristics of the return of his memories in other places repeated. The "labyrinth of alleyways" recalls his earlier spatial conception of memories "interlocking like the labyrinthine vaults" of Liverpool Street Station. And his walk through the "thoroughfares and courtyards [...] [feeling] the uneven paving [...] underfoot" leads to another central witnessing site of memory, as his nocturnal peregrinations through Greater London always led him back to Liverpool Street.[1]

Even before he meets Věra Ryšanová, who "had been my mother Agáta's neighbour and my nurserymaid" (215) and who tells him all she knows of his history and the fate of his parents, Austerlitz finds remembered fragments returning to him as a result of encountering material traces of the past – "a finely wrought window grating, the iron handle of a bell-pull, [...] the branches of an almond tree growing over a garden wall ... the smell of damp limewash, the gently rising flight of stairs [...] – all of them signs and characters from the type-case of forgotten things" (213-14). Always in *Austerlitz*, as in Sebald's other prose narratives, these are material traces encountered *in place*.

At the address he has been given by an archivist at the Prague state archives, instead of his mother, Agáta Austerlitzová, Austerlitz finds Věra and the flat in which she had lived in 1939. Significantly, like those other "places which have more of the past about them" to which Austerlitz is continually drawn, Věra's flat is "almost as it had been sixty years ago [...] because as Věra told me, said Austerlitz, once she had lost me and my mother, who was almost a sister to her, she could not bear to alter anything" (216).

The constancy of the places to which Austerlitz journeys and in which he discovers many of his lost memories by way of lingering traces of the past act as an important way to counterbalance the desperate instability of his own narrative identity. Věra has kept her flat unchanged in order to cope with the loss first of Austerlitz's father, Maximilian, who escaped

---

1 Incidentally, this motif, which intimately connects walking with the return of memory, is rehearsed in Sebald's other narratives, including in *The Rings of Saturn*. See MacDonald for a detailed discussion.

Prague for Paris just before the city was annexed by the Germans, then of Austerlitz himself when he was evacuated to England, and finally of Austerlitz's mother Agáta when she was transported to Terezín. Austerlitz's journey is characterised by his encounters with places that have the impression of being unchanged by time (although often Austerlitz discovers them and the memories they contain in the moment immediately prior to their destruction), places in which he has some hope of accessing, through his senses and the movement of his remembering body through space, long buried memories of his personal history and identity. The exception to this rule is the new Bibliothèque Nationale in Paris, which I will discuss in detail below. The waiting-room at Liverpool Street Station is described as having "obviously been disused for years" (189), Věra's flat is "almost as it had been sixty years ago," as a result of which Austerlitz experiences a glimmer of constancy ("throughout my entire life, all this had stayed in one place" [216]), and en route to Terezín, to which he travels during this visit to Prague, Austerlitz describes "a petrochemicals plant [...], with clouds of smoke rising from its cooking towers and chimneys, as they must have done without cease for many years" (263).

At the fortified town of Terezín, where there is no evidence of the population said to reside there, it is in objects displayed in the window of the Antikos Bazar that Austerlitz experiences a sense of time unchanged. Of these objects, which he spends considerable time inspecting and later describing to the narrator, Austerlitz says:

They were all as timeless as that moment of rescue, perpetuated but for ever just occurring, these ornaments, utensils and momentoes stranded in the Terezín bazaar, objects that for reasons one could never know had outlived their former owners and survived the process of destruction, so that I could now see my own faint shadow image barely perceptible among them. (276-77)

But there is a sense in which the reader can know the reasons these objects have "outlived their former owners and survived the process of destruction" (277). Austerlitz's fascination with and lengthy description of the objects in the windows of the Antikos Bazar follows Věra's retelling of the German's systematic confiscation of the Jewish population's valuables and the fundamental role played by objects in the dispossession and exile of Jewish people in areas annexed by Germany. These stories underscore the role objects play as living traces of the past in the gradual emergence of Austerlitz's memories and the re-composition of his narrative identity. "I think it was in the late autumn of 1941, said Věra, that Agáta had to take her wireless, her gramophone and the records she loved so much, her binoculars and opera glasses, musical instruments, jewellery, furs and the clothes Maximilian had left behind to the so-called Compulsory Collection Centre" (249-50). Later, when Agáta is "summoned" for transportation from Prague, Věra tells Austerlitz that she was given

> a sheaf of printed forms and instructions setting out everything down to the very smallest detail: [...] what items of clothing were to be brought – coat, raincoat, warm headgear, ear muffs, mittens, nightdress, underclothes, and so on – what articles of personal use it was advisable to bring, for instance sewing things, leather grease, a spirit stove and candles [...] what else could be brought in the way of hand baggage and provisions; [...] the proviso that [...] it was not permitted to bring cushions or other articles of furnishing, or to make rucksacks and travelling bags out of Persian rugs, winter coats, or other valuable remnants of fabric, furthermore that matches, lighters and smoking were prohibited at the embarkation point and thereafter in general. (250-51)

Immediately following Agáta's transportation, Věra further relates that

> a man from the Trusteeship Centre for Requisitioned Goods [...] put a paper seal on the doors [of her flat]. Then, between Christmas and the New Year, a troop of shady characters arrived to clear away everything that had been left behind, the furniture, the lamps and candelabra, the carpets and curtains, the books and musical scores, the clothes from the wardrobes and drawers, the bed linen, pillows, eiderdowns, blankets, china and kitchen utensils, the pot plants and umbrellas, even the bottled pears and cherries which had been standing forgotten in the cellar for years, and the remaining potatoes. They took everything, down to the very last spoon, off to one of the over fifty depots, where these abandoned objects were itemized separately with the thoroughness peculiar to the Germans, were valued, then washed, cleaned or mended as necessary, and finally stored, row upon row, on specially made shelves. (254-56)

Towards the close of Austerlitz's narrative, the reader is reminded once more of the significance ascribed to objects by the Germans, and by

Austerlitz in his quest for material traces of the past. This time in Paris, to which Austerlitz has travelled in search of traces of his father, from the eighteenth floor of the Bibliothèque Nationale, Austerlitz looks out over the city and is told by his friend and librarian, Henri Lemoine, that the new library building stands upon "waste land [where] there stood until the end of the war an extensive warehousing complex to which the Germans brought all the loot they had taken from the homes of the Jews of Paris" (401).

It is impossible to overestimate the importance of *material* traces of the past in Sebald's writing and especially in his composition of Austerlitz's memory and narrative identity. Objects such as those in the windows of the Antikos Bazar at Terezín – an inventory of which recalls those in the previous quotations – are at once a trigger that evoke repressed memories (Austerlitz is especially attracted to a "stuffed squirrel [...] whose Czech name – *veverka* – I now recalled like the name of a long-lost friend" [275-76]) and material evidence, an alternative archive of sorts, of the systematic transportation, ghettoization, and destruction of millions of people across Europe. The objects in the Antikos Bazar can be understood as their material remains.

Sebald's work is characterised by the encounter of material traces of the past – as catalysts that bring to the surface repressed memories, as evidence – *in place*. At Terezín, having finally moved away from the window of the Antikos Bazar, Austerlitz relates that "I found myself" at the Ghetto Museum (277). And it is here, moving among

> the display panels, sometimes skimming over the captions, sometimes reading them letter by letter, [staring] at the photographic reproductions [...] [that] for the first time [I] acquired some idea of the history of the persecution which my avoidance system had kept from me for so long, and which now, *in this place* surrounded me on all sides. (278, emphasis added)

History and memory are found in place and experienced by means of encounters with material traces in which the past persists in the present and through which Austerlitz, Sebald, and his readers are able to engage in an "historical metaphysic" that brings past events "back to life." Austerlitz conceives of events-in-time as ongoing, not in a linear sense but as co-existing, as persisting in place, in such a way that we can "turn back and go behind them" in order to "keep appointments in the past." For Austerlitz, events-in-time-and-place are consistent in a way that memory and narrative identity can never be. According to this logic, it makes sense to travel to the places where events have occurred in order to access through the senses otherwise lost memories and the identity to which those memories belong. Travelling, which is to say retracing a past passage, is in effect for Austerlitz a way of bringing the past back to life.

Following his visit to Terezín, Austerlitz tells the narrator that he came to feel that he "must retrace [the] journey from Prague to London by train" (286). It is on this journey that we encounter one of the most striking examples in Sebald's writing of the effect of (affecting) material traces of the past. The train Austerlitz takes from Prague to the Hook of Holland stops at Pilsen "for some time" (311). But, says Austerlitz to the narrator,

[a]ll I remember [...] is that I went out on the platform to photograph the capital of a cast-iron column that had touched some chord of recognition in me. What made me uneasy at the sight of it, however, was not the question of whether the complex form of the capital, now covered with a puce-tinged encrustation, had really impressed itself on my mind when I passed through Pilsen [...] in the summer of 1939, but the idea [...] that this cast-iron column, [...] might remember me and was, if I may so put it, said Austerlitz, a witness to what I could no longer recollect for myself. (311)

Here at Pilsen, on Austerlitz's journey to retrace his past passage as a method of triggering repressed memories, a reader of Sebald discovers the basis of the fundamental importance of place in his work. I have already stressed the significance of the movement of the remembering body *in* place – represented here by Austerlitz's decision to retrace the train journey he made aged four and a half. What is revealed at Pilsen by "the capital of the cast-iron column" is a sense in which the moving body might be remembered *by* place and the material traces encountered in the process of travel. Whether or not the cast-iron column does in fact remember Austerlitz remains unresolved, but the question nevertheless haunts the remainder of his journey and the recomposition of his narrative identity. Given the problem of remembering for Austerlitz, the extent to which he has developed his "avoidance system" (278) over the course of his lifetime, and the many gaps in his memory which persist and in important ways define the retrospective composition of his narrative identity as much as the discovery of his history and memories do, the potential for places and material traces to act as *witnesses* and active sites of remembering deserves further analysis: Can places and other material traces of the past remember us? And can their memory archive help to fill the void of missing, repressed, or otherwise traumatising personal as well as cultural memories?

The suggestion that traces have a memory independent of, but connected to, us is an elaboration in place of a notion of Věra's. At the time when Věra is relating to Austerlitz the aspects of his history with which she is familiar, as if by chance she comes across two photographs, one of which shows Austerlitz as a small boy, shortly before he left Prague. Presenting them to Austerlitz, Věra remarks upon

> the mysterious quality peculiar to such photographs when they surface from oblivion. One has the impression, she said, of something stirring in them, as if one caught small sighs of despair [...], as if the pictures had a memory of their own and remembered us, remembered the roles that we, the survivors, and those no longer among us had played in our former lives. (258)

As with the objects in the bazaar at Terezín, photographs seem to have a dual function (at least) in the composition of Austerlitz's history and identity via material traces of the past. As a rule, and certainly in the way that Sebald uses them, photographs are taken as a record of events with an eye to the retrospective reconstruction (or narration) of past events and an *aide de mémoire*. But like the cast-iron column at Pilsen, there is a wildness to photographs – a sense in which they cannot be contained (or constrained) by the meanings we give them. Photographs have a life of their own so to speak. As a result of this living quality, they possess the possibility of remembering us and, alongside other material traces, of bringing past events back to life.[2]

---

[2] George Kouvaros has also noted the importance of this episode and argues that "Sebald is trying to suggest [...] the capacity of a photograph to render a sense of duration that has left us behind, a duration that sweeps away all traces of life leaving only surface details and contingent elements" (409). Certainly there is a real sense in which photographs reveal what has been lost but read in the context

For Sebald, as for Ricoeur, photographs and other documents, the archives that house them, and the notions of witness and testimony that they invoke "reaches its final epistemological presupposition [in the] trace" (Ricoeur, *Time and Narrative III* 116). Sebald's writing, and the composition of Austerlitz's narrative, are deeply indebted to the institutions aligned with traces of the past – Austerlitz's travels through space and into memories are in effect made up of a series of visits to institutions such as state archives (in Prague), museums (at Greenwich in London and Terezín) and libraries (most notably the Bibliothèque Nationale in Paris). But at the same time as these institutions, and the traces they house, provide information crucial to the reconstruction of his memory and identity, Sebald is deeply suspicious of such houses of "official" histories and the memories they keep. Long has written extensively on Sebald's representation of photographs, archives and other intrinsically modern institutions. For him,

> The archive [...] lives at the very heart of Sebald's narrative project. His work is profoundly concerned with the material and infrastructural basis of knowledge systems, and his narrators spend an inordinate amount of time in museums and galleries, libraries and archives, zoos and menageries [....] In short, they are obsessed with processes of archivisation and with the places where the past has deposited traces and fragments that have been preserved and in many cases systematised, catalogued, or indexed. (11)

Long describes *Austerlitz* as Sebald's "most extensive exploration of the archive" (149), which at once depends for its composition upon the material housed in archival institutions, and is deeply critical of the obsessive, systematisation of information, with its intimate connection to persecution and dispossession. For Long, "the psychodrama at the heart of *Austerlitz* is a drama of the archive" (163).

The most explicit criticism of archival institutions (and the monumental history they invest in) comes in the form of Austerlitz's reflection upon the building of the new Bibliothèque Nationale in Paris. Austerlitz's narration of his ongoing search for traces of his personal history and identity comes

---

of Austerlitz's "going behind," I am less inclined to limit their function (or the function of other material traces) to "surface details."

to a close (but by no means an end) in Paris where he has travelled "to search for traces of his father's movements, and to transport himself back to the time when he too had lived there" (254). Always, for Austerlitz, travel through space is travel (back) in time.

All of Austerlitz's powers as an architectural historian come to bear on his description of the new Bibliothèque Nationale. He argues that this building has been designed to cut contemporary readers off from traces of the past. Indeed, the building is in an important sense concealing evidence of past atrocities. For Austerlitz, its "monumental dimension" is "unwelcoming if not inimical to human beings" (386). The entrance "must have been devised – I can think of no other explanation, said Austerlitz – on purpose to instil a sense of insecurity and humiliation in the poor reader" (389). Once inside the library, Austerlitz tells the narrator,

I came to the conclusion that in any project we design and develop, the size and degree of complexity of the information and control systems inscribed in it are the crucial factors, so that the all-embracing and absolute perfection of the concept can in practice coincide, indeed must ultimately coincide, with its chronic dysfunction and constitutional instability. At any rate, […] I for my part, said Austerlitz, found this gigantic new library, which according to one of the loathsome phrases now current is supposed to serve as the treasure-house of our entire literary heritage, proved useless in my search for any traces of my father who had disappeared from Paris more than fifty years ago. (392-93)

The implied comparison between the Bibliothèque Nationale's complex "information and control systems" and the systems put into place in German-occupied territories during the war to control Jewish and other persecuted populations is palpable. Both systems instil a sense of insecurity and humiliation; both are, it seems clear, designed to work *against* memory and access to living traces of the past. There is an obvious criticism here of "heritage" and the "monumental" which is implicitly compared with the notions of personal and cultural histories, the memories and material traces from which they are composed, and the pivotal role they play in the construction of narrative identity.

What we find at this last station on Austerlitz's journey in search of traces of his past, as he relates it to the narrator, is a disturbing pronouncement of the human desire to "break with everything which still has some living connection to the past" (298). The Bibliothèque Nationale has been built on the site at which the "loot" confiscated from Parisian Jews was sorted and warehoused. As Austerlitz's friend Lemoine states, "the fact is that the whole affair is buried in the most literal sense beneath the foundations of our pharaonic President's Grande Bibliothèque" (403).

If the Bibliothèque Nationale represents the future of archival institutions then the fear is that the discovery of connections with *living* traces of the past will no longer be possible which would make the retrospective composition of personal memories and a narrative identity for someone like Austerlitz impossible. And, as Austerlitz's story demonstrates, memories accessed by way of encounters in place with material traces of the past, from which a narrative identity can be formulated, are a matter of life and death. Until he begins to remember, Austerlitz tells the narrator, I felt "I had never really been alive, or was only now being born" (193).

Austerlitz, then, is born at the moment of his encounter with living traces of the past, traces that bring the past back to life. He traces his story backwards from Liverpool Street Station by travelling to the sites of memory from which it is composed – Prague, Terezín, the train journey via Pilsen to the Hook of Holland, Paris – then recounts that journey forwards, to the narrator, with all of the insight gained in the process of reflecting *back*. This movement backwards and forwards echoes Austerlitz's conception of time as persisting in "places which have more of the past about them" (259), of events-in-time coexisting in such a way that we "can turn back and go behind" them (144), and his belief that the dead move amongst the living. Most importantly, it enables him, at the onset of old age, "almost on the eve of [his] death" to be born again at the moment of the return of memories of his childhood and to come alive through the living connection to material traces of the past as they are encountered in place.

REFERENCES

Bauer, Karin. "The Dystopian Entwinement of Histories and Identities in W. G. Sebald's *Austerlitz*." *W. G. Sebald: History – Memory – Trauma*. Ed. Scott Denham and Mark McCulloh. Berlin: de Gruyter, 2007. 233-50. Print.

Garloff, Katja. "The Task of the Narrator: Moments of Symbolic Investiture in W. G. Sebald's *Austerlitz*." *W. G. Sebald: History – Memory – Trauma*. Ed. Scott Denham and Mark McCulloh. Berlin and New York: de Gruyter, 2007. 157-69. Print.

Goodbody, Axel. "Sense of Place and Lieu de Mémoire: A Cultural Approach to Environmental Texts." *Ecocritical Theory: New European Approaches*. Ed. Axel Goodbody and Kate Rigby. Charlottesville: U of Virginia P, 2001. 55-67. Print.

Kouvaros, George. "Images that Remember Us: Photography and Memory in *Austerlitz*." *Amsterdamer Beiträge zur Neueren Germanistik* 72.1 (2009): 389-412.

Leone, Massimo. "Textual Wanderings: A Vertiginous Reading of W. G. Sebald." *W. G. Sebald: A Critical Companion*. Ed. J. J. Long and Anne Whitehead. Edinburgh: Edinburgh UP, 2004. 89-101. Print.

Long, J. J. *W. G. Sebald: Image, Archive, Modernity*. New York: Columbia UP, 2007. Print.

MacDonald, Anna. "'Pictures in the Rebus': Puzzling out W. G. Sebald's Monstrous Geographies." *Monstrous Spaces: The Other Frontier*. Ed. Niculae Liviu Gheran and Ken Monteith. Oxford: Inter-disciplinary Press, 2013. 115-25. Print.

Ricoeur, Paul. *Time and Narrative III*. Trans. Kathleen McLaughlin and David Pellauer. Chicago: U of Chicago P, 1985. Print.

---. *Time and Narrative I*. Trans. Kathleen McLaughlin and David Pellauer. Chicago: U of Chicago P, 1983. Print.

Sebald, W. G. *Austerlitz*. Trans. Anthea Bell. Harmondsworth: Penguin, 2001. Print.

Haunted by a Traumatic Past
Age, Memory, and Narrative Identity in Margaret Atwood's
The Blind Assassin

TERESA GIBERT

> "But what is a memorial, when you come right down to it, but a commemoration of wounds endured? Endured, and resented. Without memory, there can be no revenge."
> (ATWOOD, *THE BLIND ASSASSIN* 508)

The relationship between memory and the narrative construction of personal identity constitutes a major thematic concern in many of Margaret Atwood's novels, because her protagonists develop their sense of selfhood through a specific kind of storytelling which is mainly based on the twofold process of retrospection and recollection of their past experiences. This major theme of Atwood's fiction can be fruitfully explored within the conceptual framework of the theory of narrative identity expounded by Paul Ricoeur in his three-volume *Time and Narrative* (1983-1985), *Oneself as Another* (1990), and *Memory, History, Forgetting* (2000), a book in which the French philosopher asserted: "On the deepest level, that of symbolic mediation of action, it is through the narrative function that memory is incorporated into the formation of identity" (84-85).[1] The strong will to narrate *memory traces* plays a central role in *The Handmaid's Tale* (1985), *Cat's Eye* (1988), *The Robber Bride* (1993), *Alias Grace* (1996) and *The Blind Assassin* (2000), but what adds an interesting dimension to the last mentioned – the author's tenth novel – is that it focuses on how such *memory traces* function differently according to each life stage, from infancy to old age, with emphasis on the latter.

The Blind Assassin, a Booker Prize-winning novel published by Atwood when she was sixty-one, throws new light on issues of ageing through the figure of its eighty-two-year-old protagonist and first-person narrator, Iris Chase, a very creative and unusually vibrant elderly character shaped along the non-stereotypical lines of two other characters of the Canadian literary canon: ninety-year-old Hagar Shipley (Margaret Laurence, *The Stone Angel*, 1964) and eighty-year-old Daisy Goodwill Flett (Carol Shields, *The Stone Diaries*, 1993). Iris Chase reviews her life through recollections of her childhood, adolescence, and adulthood, showing how each of these phases has been affected by different ways of remembering or forgetting the episodes which have marked her evolving personality. One of the valuable assets of her wide narrative perspective stems from her longevity, which extends from 1916 to 1999, covering almost the entire twentieth century against the background of Canadian history.[2]

Iris Chase writes her memoir in the final and most productive stage of her life, from May 1998 to May 1999, racing against her biological clock with growing urgency, because she is aware of her imminent death due to her heart condition.[3] She interweaves her fragmentary autobiographical

---

1 Ricoeur summed up his notion of narrative identity as follows: "The narrative constructs the identity of the character, what can be called his or her narrative identity, in constructing that of the story told. It is the identity of the story that makes the identity of the character" (*Oneself as Another* 147-48).

2 Dvorak has examined how national and international events intersect with domestic history in *The Blind Assassin*.

3 Near the middle of her memoir, Iris remarks: "I hasten on, making my way crabwise across the paper. It's a slow race now, between me and my heart, but I intend to get there first. Where is there? The end, or *The End*. One or the other. Both are destinations, of a sort" (222-23). Alison Reed contends that the

account of past events with numerous diary-like acerbic comments about her present decaying existence while often musing on the pervasive effects of the passage of time on her ability to remember. For example, being anxious that people might notice any visible signs of her mental decline during a high school graduation ceremony, Iris confesses her fear to seem "forgetful" in front of her hometown audience (39). Since she finds no way to shirk her participation, she faces the challenge reluctantly and ends up feeling dissatisfied with her public performance. Having spent most of her time on the stage daydreaming in her chair and missing much of what is going on, at the crucial moment of presenting the Laura Chase Memorial Prize in honour of her late sister, she has an episode of confusion and wonders hesitantly: "Now what had I been intending to say?" (41).

On another occasion, near the end of her memoir, Iris analyses with ironic detachment how the meaning of the word *escarpment* has suddenly eluded her: "Today my brain dealt me a sudden blank; a whiteout, as if by snow. It wasn't someone's name that disappeared – in any case that's usual – but a word, which turned itself upside down and emptied itself of meaning like a cardboard cup blown over" (490). Her resorting to two conspicuous similes and her thorough explanation of the incident in three short paragraphs indicate her desire to draw attention to this disruption in her semantic memory system rather than trying to hide it. She recognises that this weakness may interfere with her writing aims, but far from being deterred, persistent and resourceful Iris demonstrates that she can easily circumvent the problem by consulting a dictionary.

Moreover, Iris acknowledges her memory failures in various other manners, always highlighting them. Sometimes she simply uses phrases such as "I can't remember when, exactly" (99) or "I can't recall" (173) whenever she is unable to report relatively unimportant details. On one occasion, after giving notice that she does not know something for certain, she speculates about what may have happened, but then she suddenly remembers and proposes for acceptance a version which wholly contradicts the one she has just offered (285). This example illustrates how *memory*

---

protagonist of *The Blind Assassin* "draws attention to her aging body as narrator" (21), and that "the narrative tension is sustained, most prominently" by the aging body of Iris, "whose own foreseeable death might preempt the conclusion" (22).

traces can resurface if they have temporarily been "rendered inaccessible, unavailable" in what Ricoeur calls the "reserve of forgetting" rather than "definitively erased" (*Memory* 416, 428).

After a long digression for which Iris apologises and which she attributes to people's tendency to indulge in "apocalyptic visions" when they become old, she continues: "For a moment I've lost the thread, it's hard for me to remember, but then I do" (478). Other, more significant types of memory breakdown she carefully records are those not directly related to senility but to the impact of her traumatic experiences on her memory, starting with the early loss of her beloved mother. The elderly Iris elaborates at length on how she, as a nine-year-old girl, had been so greatly distressed by her mother's demise that, shortly after it, she had to make an effort to recall "the exact forms" which her grief had taken or what she had "done on the day Mother died" (142). Many decades later, Iris contends that in those hours of bereavement she already had to rely on photographs, because she could hardly remember what her mother had really looked like in spite of the fact that she had just lost her. Pondering on the physical traces of her then recently deceased mother – the empty bed, the afternoon light falling so silently across the hardwood floor, and the aroma still lingering in the room – Iris underscores how at that distant time she "could remember her absence [...] much better than her presence" (142).[4]

Furthermore, while providing evidence of her disastrous paternally arranged marriage of convenience, Iris claims to have forgotten almost everything about her wedding, which was her next traumatic experience, signalling her break with adolescence at the age of eighteen exactly as her childhood had abruptly ended at the age of nine with the death of her mother. Her statement "Speeches were made, of which I remember nothing" (240) may not come as a surprise, but what seems astonishing is her insistence on the obliteration of any reminiscences which might link her present self to that of her past self embodied by the young bride she contemplates in her own wedding photograph. Devoting one full page to

---

4 In her psychoanalytic study of *The Blind Assassin*, Ruth Parkin-Gounelas highlights the visual dimensions of this novel, which emphasises "memory as retro-spection in the literal sense of looking back" (681). Her perceptive observation that "within Atwood's narrative, material objects function as markers of loss" can be applied to this passage (685).

the picture, Iris allots the first two paragraphs to a rather harsh description of the bride and a no less sarcastic fourth paragraph to that of the bridegroom. Between them, she inserts the following third paragraph, enclosed in parentheses, in order to comment on the bride with whom she no longer identifies:

(I say "her," because I don't recall having been present, not in any meaningful sense of the word. I and the girl in the picture have ceased to be the same person. I am her outcome, the result of the life she once lived headlong; whereas she, if she can be said to exist at all, is composed only of what I remember. I have the better view – I can see her clearly, most of the time. But even if she knew enough to look, she can't see me at all.) (239)

This compelling parenthetical aside conveys the protagonist's perception of herself as if there were two completely different people engaged in her writing process: her *remembering self* (the octogenarian Iris speculating on her wedding photograph) and one of her former *remembered selves* (the eighteen-year-old Iris represented in the photograph).[5] This passage also illustrates to what extent Iris is aware of the high mobility of personal identity, which is never immutable or fixed in time, as Ricoeur convincingly argued.[6]

According to what Iris asserts in her old age, there are other disturbing areas in which her memory seems to have malfunctioned all through her life, particularly at times of crisis, although there is ample proof that her ability to remember was never so faulty as she declares it to be. For

---

5 This passage illustrates Ulric Neisser's following point: "The self that is remembered today is not the historical self of yesterday, but only a reconstructed version. A different version – a new remembered self – may be reconstructed tomorrow" (8). According to Murray Schwartz, "aging normally generates a multiplicity of self-images" (3).

6 In "Reflections on a New Ethos for Europe" Ricoeur observed that "narrative identity is not that of an immutable substance or of a fixed structure, but rather the mobile identity issuing from the combination of the concordance of the story, taken as a structured totality, and the discordance imposed by the encountered events. Alternatively put, narrative identity takes part in the mobility of the story, in its dialectic of order and disorder" (6).

example, during her unhappy honeymoon, when she finally walked on the deck after having been seasick for three days while crossing from New York to Europe, she felt deeply disappointed both at what the ocean really looked like and at her difficulty in establishing any literary connections with what was supposed to be a delightful view: "I tried to remember something I might have read about it, some poem or other, but could not" (246). However, after mentioning those brief moments of memory loss, she adds what she immediately called up: *"Break, break, break*. Something began that way. It had cold grey stones in it. *Oh Sea"* (246). Thus, she shows that in fact she remembered at least the first two lines of one of Lord Tennyson's poems which she had learned as a child and previously quoted in her memoir: "Break, break, break, / On thy cold gray stones, O Sea!" (156). This elegy, written by Alfred Tennyson in memory of his friend Arthur Hallam, was exactly in tune with Iris's grieving state of mind, and it was the only poem she evoked because it mirrored her gloomy thoughts.[7] Although the prevailing emotion in this particular passage is sorrow, the elderly Iris notes further in her confessional memoir that the emotion she now recalls most clearly from the eight weeks of her honeymoon is "anxiety" (300).

When revisiting her past, Iris sometimes expresses her reluctance to remember, and unequivocally argues that memory "can turn you rancid" (508). Some occurrences of apparent memory failure epitomise her desire to forget, that is, her will to create a type of memory which is not intent on remembering everything, but attempts to destroy certain traumatic *memory traces* and succeeds to a varying degree in achieving this therapeutic goal. The advantages of forgetfulness are evoked by one of her interlocutors in direct allusion to the erasure of the painful wartime memories of his orphaned childhood in a ravaged country in Eastern Europe (189). Iris's first recorded memory is also related to the Great War, but as she was living safely in Canada, far away from the battle zones, what she recalls is a pleasant flashback of Armistice Day. She describes in synaesthetic terms how, on 11 November 1918, the chilly air in the garden of Avilion was

---

7   In her detailed analysis of the intertextual character of *The Blind Assassin*, Andrea Strolz draws attention to the relevance of the Victorian cultural context in this novel (*Escaping from the Prison-House* 112), and discusses in particular the protagonist's use of Lord Tennyson's poem (127-29).

filled with the sound of the church bells ringing, there was frost on the fallen leaves, and in the middle of this idyllic scene, she broke with a stick a skim of ice on the lily pond (75).

Throughout her memoir Iris devotes a great deal of attention to the memories of her early childhood, which are inextricably associated with Avilion, the most important place she ever inhabited and the one that left an indelible mark on her psyche.[8] Avilion shapes both her individual memory and the collective memory of three generations as well, so that it is not a mere place which all of them remember, but becomes a genuine *place of memory*, standing out as a mute witness of the Chase family history, from their prosperity to their ruin. As a child, Iris was perceptive enough to realise that the house where she was born still reverberated with the people who once lived there, starting with her grandmother, Adelia, who had supervised its planning and decoration until its completion in the year 1899 (59-60). Priding herself on her elegant taste, Adelia took the name of Avilion from Tennyson's *Morte d'Arthur* and printed five lines of his poem – already outmoded in England by then – on her Christmas cards, an emblematic gesture of her social and cultural pretensions (61). When Iris was about thirteen or fourteen, she used to romanticise the glamorous figure of Adelia, whom she had never met, but whose exemplary life she reconstructed by gathering information from various sources, including her scrapbooks (158, 389) and portraits (59, 168), some anecdotes told by the housekeeper Reenie (63-64), and the imprint left by the long dead woman

---

8   Arguing that the inhabiting of physical places is crucial to the recovery of memory, Paul Ricoeur notes: "The transition from corporeal memory to the memory of places is assured by acts as important as orientating oneself, moving from place to place, and above all inhabiting. [...] This way, the 'things' remembered are intrinsically associated with places" (*Memory* 41). According to Ricoeur, "[p]laces inhabited are memorable par excellence" (*Memory* 42). Ricoeur further stresses the relationship between inhabited places and both individual memory and collective memory when he observes: "The memory of having inhabited some house in some town or that of having traveled in some part of the world are particularly eloquent and telling. They weave together an intimate memory and one shared by those close to one" (*Memory* 148). Avilion provides the spatial dimension which enables the transition from Iris's individual memory to the collective memory of her relatives.

on the mansion she had designed and no one dared to renovate (62). After her death in 1913, Adelia's presence in the Chase ancestral home continued to be so overwhelming that Iris, born three years later, grew up under the impression of "being brought up by her" (62). Thus, Avilion mediates the intersection between Iris's individual identity and that of Adelia, who left behind many *memory traces* of her thoughts and actions, as reflected in the education of her three sons, christened Norval, Edgar and Percival, according to her idea of suitable "high-toned" names (62). Curiously enough, Adelia's arranged marriage to Benjamin Chase would be replicated by that of Iris to Richard Griffen. Just as Adelia "wasn't married" but "married off" – in Reenie's words – by her respectable but impoverished family (59), her son Norval would "marry off" Iris to the wealthy businessman Richard Griffen in an attempt to save the Chase properties from bankruptcy. Although all the Chase possessions were part of that financial agreement, it is significant that Norval Chase did not mention the button factory, their main source of revenue, but only Avilion, "mortgaged up to the hilt," hence resorting to emotional blackmail as a means of pressuring his daughter into marrying Richard (226).

Partly due to the declining family fortune, Avilion lost its lustre, later became a summer residence for Iris and her husband (when the couple lived in Toronto), began to fall apart after their divorce, and at last was "sadly transformed" into an old-age home inaptly renamed Valhalla (57). Although the elderly Iris states that she has never been inside the house since it was converted to its new use, she supposes that "it reeks no doubt of baby powder and sour urine and day-old boiled potatoes" (57). In one of her nightmares she sees an even worse image of Avilion, with its "ruined glass conservatory" full of dead plants and its main house "dark, deserted" (329). Therefore, she would "rather remember it the way it was," even though "shabbiness was already setting in" at the time she knew it (57). When Iris was a child, Avilion was characterised by "its obsolete Victorian splendours, its air of aesthetic decay, of departed grace, of wan regret" (157). At present, she defines as "ambition's mausoleum" the rich "merchant's palace" that Avilion was in its prime (58).[9] Although she never

---

9   Susan Strehle notes how "Atwood emphasizes the pretentiousness of Avilion, which aspires to confer upper class dignity and antiquity on new button-manufacturing money" (10).

was a first-hand witness of the glorious period when three Canadian Prime Ministers stayed at Avilion while visiting Port Ticonderoga, she relies on the cross-generational oral transmission of such events and on the photographs attesting to them (60).[10]

The second most important *place of memory* in *The Blind Assassin* is the local First World War Memorial, a pyramid built with rounded river stones like the ones used for the construction of Avilion, topped by the statue of a "dejected-looking" Weary Soldier (148). Iris first mentions this *site of memory* when she briefly describes the photo of her "father with a wreath, in front of the War Memorial at its dedication" (51) among a series of "giant blow-ups of old photos from the town archives" decorating the walls of the modern shopping centre into which Chase button factory has been converted (50). Later, the octogenarian's memories are elicited again, though they are not sparked by a photograph, but by the actual sight of the monument during a walk in the town centre. On this occasion, she recalls the history of the memorial and describes it very thoroughly in the chapter entitled "The Weary Soldier" (144-51). In this section of her memoir, Iris gives a detailed account of the bitter controversy provoked when her father, Captain Norval Chase, a seriously maimed WWI veteran eager to honour the memory of his two brothers and that of his fallen comrades, made sure that the monument he was sponsoring reflected a glimpse of the horrors of warfare rather than suit the conventional views of the majority of the citizens of Port Ticonderoga, who would have preferred the more triumphant symbol of a Goddess of Victory. The arguments about the inscription ended with Captain Chase imposing the motto "Lest We Forget" (148), a phrase drawn from the oft-repeated line in Rudyard Kipling's "Recessional" (1897) which the poet himself chose as one of the memorial formulae for the battlefield cemeteries when he became the literary advisor of the Imperial War Graves Commission (Renard 304). Iris records how she

---

10 Shuli Barzilai analyzes the various purposes of "phototextuality" in *The Blind Assassin*, rightly pointing out that all of the photographs in this novel "are fictional constructs" which are "presented in realistic terms" (106). It should be noted that Port Ticonderoga itself is a fictional town which is also described realistically and that, according to Atwood, it is a blend of four Ontario towns: Stratford, Saint Mary's, Elora, and Paris ("Margaret Atwood on *The Blind Assassin*").

and her sister attended the unveiling on Remembrance Day 1928 and expounds the effects that the moving ceremony had on both children, as shown by the ensuing dialogue between Laura and her nursemaid. Back home, to young Laura's question about why the monument was called a memorial, Reenie answered that it was meant for the living to remember the dead, adding that in fact the memorial was more intended for the former than for the latter (150), a notion obsessively internalised by Iris who, very much like her father, would end up being overwhelmed by what Ricoeur calls "the frenzy of commemoration" (*Memory* 85, 90).

The chapter entitled "The Weary Soldier" contains only some of the numerous references to the phenomenon of memorializing to be found in *The Blind Assassin*. Other instances of this recurrent motif appear in the form of quotations from a popular poem about remembering the WWI dead, John McCrae's "In Flanders Fields" (1915), which had a lasting impact on Canada's collective memory. Iris quotes its first two lines – *"In Flanders fields the poppies blow, Between the crosses, row on row"* – when she gives examples of the literary works she used to read in her grandfather's library (155). Subsequently she cites one line from its last stanza – *"To you from failing hands we throw"* – to conclude one of her later chapters, ending with a poignant image of the "hungry ghosts" of the dead by whom she feels haunted (508).

The experience of war is recurrently related to issues of remembrance all through *The Blind Assassin* not only by means of remarks about Port Ticonderoga's War Memorial and intertextual allusions to "In Flanders Fields," but also by a direct reference to the memory loss suffered by Iris's grandfather as one of the many negative consequences of the Great War upon the Chase family. Benjamin Chase "had a devastating stroke, which affected his speech and his memory" shortly after he learned that two of his three sons had been killed, one at the Ypres Salient and the other at the Somme (73). Unlike Dr. Simon Jordan, the military surgeon who lost his memory as a result of injuries sustained during the American Civil War in *Alias Grace*, in *The Blind Assassin* Captain Norval Chase's wounds seem to have enhanced his ability to remember the First World War to the point that his constant dwelling upon it becomes a pathological obsession which damages his life and that of his wife and his two daughters. Iris intuits that her father had suffered from a morbid condition when she recalls how he used to gaze out of the window absentmindedly, and surmises that he might have been "feeling a certain nostalgia for the war, despite its stench and meaningless carnage" (81). Although Iris did not witness that war firsthand, she inherited her father's remembrance of it through a process of memory transmission across generations which can be described in terms of Marianne Hirsch's concept of "postmemory" (106).[11]

Iris realises that being a direct witness to events does not always guarantee truthfulness and explicitly questions the accuracy of her memory when she asks herself: "[I]s what I remember the same thing as what actually happened?" (217). As her memoir progresses, it becomes increasingly obvious that her memories can be neither verified nor discredited. In addition to casting doubts upon the reliability of her memory, she renders suspect her own reliability as a narrator and does so on purpose, because whenever she addresses the topic of the blurring of boundaries between truth and fiction, she makes readers wonder whether all the recollections in her narrative are trustworthy, or if some of them may be false.[12] She even announces that she is withholding information: "I look back over what I've written and I know it's wrong, not because of what I've set down, but because of what I've omitted" (395). Taking into account that she shows signs of being an unreliable narrator – actually "a liar" in Atwood's words – we are encouraged to consider to what extent certain episodes may be either the result of her deteriorating memory, or else the wilful lies Iris devises not only to justify herself, but also to assuage her feelings of guilt, especially in matters pertaining to her responsibility for her sister's suicide.[13] The frequent alternation between her declarations of self-vindication and those of self-reproach when telling the details and

---

11 "Postmemory describes the relationship that the generation after those who witnessed cultural or collective trauma bears to the experiences of those who came before, experiences that they 'remember' only by means of the stories, images, and behaviors among which they grew up" (Hirsch 106).

12 In her review of *The Blind Assassin*, Elaine Showalter remarked that Iris is "obsessed with memory and truth, but is wildly unreliable and secretive" (53). Natalie Cooke justly formulated the following paradox that, "the more Atwood's narrators admit their unreliability, the more reliable they seem to become" (208).

13 Atwood mentioned her protagonist's propensity for lying: "But my Iris Chase was predestined to be a liar, at least in matters that concerned her dead sister, Laura" ("Margaret Atwood on *The Blind Assassin*").

interpreting what may or may not have happened conveys a multi-layered richness to her complex and deliberately ambiguous narrative.

The dynamic relationship between amnesia and truth telling plays a prominent role in *Alias Grace*, where it is the key to determining whether the protagonist of the novel is innocent or guilty of the murders for which she was convicted and imprisoned. Unlike Grace Marks, Iris Chase needs neither feign amnesia nor allege real amnesia so as not to be condemned for being her sister's assassin.[14] Iris casts herself as *The Blind Assassin* of the novel's title by asserting that she had been "so blind" that she did not realise how her husband had been sexually abusing her nervous younger sister (500).[15] Along with emphasizing her metaphorical blindness, Iris portrays herself as an assassin when she explains how, acting out of spite, she drove her sensitive sister to suicide in 1945 by unexpectedly breaking to her two terrible pieces of news: that Alex Thomas, the man with whom Laura was infatuated, had been killed in the war, and that he had been Iris's lover (488).[16] Apart from manifesting that she hurt Laura voluntarily by telling

---

14 Coral Ann Howells discusses the phenomenon of amnesia in *Alias Grace* and compares it with the unearthing of secrets in *The Blind Assassin* (40-42). Contrasting these two novels, Earl G. Ingersoll points out that while in *Alias Grace* "readers grow less confident that the truth of Grace's culpability can ever be determined, *The Blind Assassin* seems to be offering a narrative in which the truth will ultimately be revealed" (548-49).

15 At this point, readers may conclude that Iris has turned a blind eye on the sexual abuse perpetrated by her husband in the same manner that she had previously ignored little Laura's complaints about being molested by Mr. Erskine, their sadistic teacher (165).

16 Gillet (16), Ingersoll (550), Michael (98), Robinson (353), Stein ("Margaret Atwood's *The Blind Assassin*" 34), Strolz (*Escaping from the Prison-House* 134-35), and Watkins (235) assume that the blind assassin in the title of the novel is Iris Chase, apart from the professional blind assassin hired by the lord of the underworld to kill the king in the inner science-fiction story within "The Blind Assassin." According to Barbara Dancygier, "Alex emerges as an even better candidate for the role" of the "blind assassin" (146). In addition to Iris, J. Brooks Bouson also identifies Richard, Iris's husband, as another "blind assassin" in the sense that he is "a ruthless man who brutally violates Laura even as he turns 'too blind an eye' to Germany's 'brutal violations of democracy'

her something she knew her mentally fragile sister was unable to bear, Iris reveals the precise memory which triggered her violent reaction. Closing her eyes for a moment, she pictured a scene at Avilion from the day after their mother's funeral, when she had pushed Laura off the ledge of the lily pond onto the grass in order to shake her complacent assurance about heaven (487). In other words, rather than linking the assassination to amnesia, as the protagonist of *Alias Grace* does, Iris connects it to remembrance. One flashback exemplifying the early sibling rivalry between the sisters is the specific memory that twenty years later overcomes Iris and leads her to perform the lethal act of cruelty which would "haunt" her for the rest of her life (488). At the beginning of her memoir, when Iris reviewed that episode of their childhood, she admitted that at the age of nine she had felt gratified by making her six-year-old sister suffer as much as she was suffering at the time of their mother's death (97).[17] On the contrary, at the end of her memoir, Iris completes her self-accusation by expressing bitter regret over her part in inducing the suicide of her heartbroken sister, whom she likens to a sleepwalker killed by the shock of being woken up (488). Although Iris also refers to many other factors contributing to Laura's decision, she blames herself for being the one who metaphorically awakened her vulnerable sister, and foregrounds the importance of this

---

(480)" (266). Sharon Rose Wilson considers that Iris is not the only one, but "one of the novel's many *Blind Assassins*" ("Blindness and Survival" 185). Barzilai contends that "Norval Chase is a strong candidate for nomination as *the* blind assassin" (114). In "A Left-Handed Story" Stein points out that "Norval Chase epitomizes blindness, for he returns from the war with one blind eye he covers with a patch" (145), and apart from identifying Iris as the "blind assassin," she also signals "time itself" as another "sinister assassin" (150). Likewise, Strolz calls attention to the "assassinating" power of time, "the devourer of all things" in Ovid's words ("'True Stories' in the Course of Time" 302, 305).

17 Fiona Tolan has explored Atwood's problematic depiction of sisterhood by focusing on the difficult sisterly relations between Iris and Laura in the context of the author's (post)feminist concerns.

tragic event in the very first sentence of her memoir: "Ten days after the war ended, my sister Laura drove a car off a bridge" (1).[18]

Filled with remorse, two years after her sister's suicide, in 1947 Iris publishes a novel purportedly written by Laura. The text of this novel or novella, also entitled "The Blind Assassin," is interpolated into the confessional memoir which constitutes the frame story of *The Blind Assassin*, chapter by chapter, as a book-within-a-book.[19] It is not until the last pages of the book that Iris avows that the embedded romance was authored by herself, rather than by Laura. This plot twist entails a complete reinterpretation of the largely autobiographical content of "The Blind Assassin," about which readers have been intentionally misled. At the beginning of her memoir, long before she proclaims her authorship, Iris reflects on her concern about her sister's immortal renown: "It's only the book that makes her memorable now" (46). Even after the disclosure of her secret, Iris continues to give the impression that her main reason for posthumously attributing her own work to Laura was that she wanted to turn her dead sister into a famous novelist by constructing a literary memorial in her honour, as an act of atonement. Readers assume beyond any shadow of a doubt that the romance entitled "The Blind Assassin" is a memorial for Laura when Iris observes:

Officially, Laura had been papered over. A few years more and it would be almost as if she'd never existed. I shouldn't have taken a vow of silence, I told myself. What did I want? Nothing much. Just a memorial of some kind. But what is a memorial, when you come right down to it, but a commemoration of wounds endured? Endured, and resented. Without memory, there can be no revenge. (508)

---

18 In her extremely suggestive discussion of the *narrative anchors* of Atwood's novel, Barbara Dancygier stresses how "the choice of the verb *drive* implies agenthood, and, consequently, intentional behavior, so that it is unlikely that Laura's death was a result of an accident" (138).

19 Most critics refer to the embedded novel or novella presumably written by Laura as "The Blind Assassin" in order to distinguish it from Atwood's complete novel, although the author never uses such quotation marks, but italicises its title when she refers to it throughout *The Blind Assassin* either to present its chapters or to mention the 1947 edition of the book (283, 287, 435, 498, 509).

But, a few pages below, Iris finally clarifies her stance when she affirms that she began "The Blind Assassin" because she "wanted a memorial" for her lover Alex and for herself as well (512), and ends up revealing her additional reasons for ascribing to Laura the authorship of this popular romance. Iris explains that she wrote it during her "long evenings alone" while she was waiting for Alex to come back from the war and continued after she knew he had been killed in the campaign to liberate Holland (512). She vindicates her usual blurring of boundaries between fact and fancy when she openly substantiates her prime intention: to record "what I remembered and also what I imagined, which is also the truth" (512). Acknowledging that hiding herself behind her sister's name could be interpreted as either "cowardice" or "simple prudence," Iris points out that it was also a matter of "justice" because in a "spiritual sense" Laura had been her "collaborator" (512-13).[20] By uncovering the buried memories of her extramarital affair in "The Blind Assassin" and attributing this autobiographical book to Laura, Iris performed the act of revenge against her abusive husband she intimated in her phrase, "Without memory, there can be no revenge" (508). The proof that Iris succeeded in avenging her sister lies first in her destruction of Richard Griffen's political career as a result of the scandal ensuing from the publication of the book and ultimately in his suicide, provoked by his inability to cope with his false suspicion – bolstered by the plot of the romance – that Laura (with whom he had been "besotted") and Alex had been lovers (510).[21] This steadfast connection between memory and revenge in Atwood's novel can be set in contrast with Ricoeur's equally persistent linking of memory and forgiveness, as exemplified in his extensive reflections on how forgetting can either permit or prevent forgiveness (*Memory* 457-506). But rather than associating her duty to remember (*le devoir de mémoire*) with the possibility of forgiving the "wounds endured," Iris is still so angry that she couples such duty exclusively with her firm will to take revenge (508).

---

20 Alice Ridout has thoroughly explored the implications of this co-authorship (18).
21 In "Talking Back to Bluebeard" Karen F. Stein states that "Iris Chase Griffen tells her story in an intricately layered text that provides her the means of escaping from her abusive husband and avenging herself on him" (165).

The proper names of the two protagonists of "The Blind Assassin," who pursue a passionate love affair, are never mentioned. Instead, the two unnamed lovers are referred to throughout the embedded novel via third person pronouns. There is no confusion about the identity of the male lover, because at some point in her memoir Iris remarks that she and her sister never referred to Alex by his name, but simply as *he*: "Alex Thomas never needed a name, for Laura: he was always *he, him, his*" (393). As for the female lover, readers are led to believe that she is Laura until they come near the end of *The Blind Assassin*, when they learn that the author of "The Blind Assassin" is not Laura, but Iris.

The fact that the frame story (written in the first person) and the embedded romance (written in the third person) are both authored by Iris justifies certain similarities in the treatment of issues of remembrance in the two narratives, inspired by an identical obsession with memory. Yet there are differences in her approach, some of which can be linked to the fact that she wrote the frame story in her early eighties whereas she created the embedded story when she was about thirty years old. Moreover, the prologue of the romance novel she published under her sister's name emphasised the youth of its author by stating that Laura had written it "before the age of twenty-five" (509). The elderly Iris writing her memoir in 1998-1999 is engrossed in reviewing her past life and tends to look backwards. By contrast, more than fifty years earlier, the young Iris writing the romance novel is totally immersed in a love affair, and therefore she speaks about memory while enjoying the present and still looking forward to the future. Hence, it seems suitable that the female protagonist of the romance novel published in 1947 should express her desire to efface her sad souvenirs – exercising a sort of "happy forgetting" cultivated within the context of an *ars oblivionis* instead of an *ars memoriae* (Ricoeur, *Memory* 503) – and seek the soothing forgetfulness which only her lover can provide: "She goes to him for amnesia, for oblivion. She renders herself up, is blotted out; enters the darkness of her own body, forgets her name" (261). In bed with her lover, she asserts her wish to seize the pleasurable present so as to be able to retrieve it sometime in the future but immediately wonders why she is so concerned with such anticipation of her nostalgia yet to come: "I will always remember this, she tells herself. Then: Why am I thinking about memory? It's not *then* yet, it's now. It's not over" (341). When her lover asks her if she will really remember what he is telling her, she assures him hastily, "I remember every word you say" (341). Later on, pondering on his absence, she still conceptualises memory in a favourable light, as a place of "refuge" where she feels sheltered, and as her favourite "pastime," because she likes to spend her afternoons recalling him rather than "passing the time" with other activities such as "the swimming pool, the quoits, the badminton, the endless, pointless games" (349). Musing about her missing lover, she vividly imagines him returning from the war on a long journey by train and safely arriving at the railway station. But at the precise moment of fantasizing about their reunion on the platform, which can be interpreted as an idealised version of Captain Norval Chase's miserable homecoming at the end of WWI (76), she fails to see her lover distinctly enough: "But her mind can't hold him, she can't fix the memory of what he looks like" (413). This intensely visual imaginary scene – never materialised – illustrates the mysterious vagaries of memory related to the elusive bodies of people who no longer belong to this world and, replicating Iris's difficulty to remember her dead mother's physical appearance soon after her passing away (142), functions as a foreshadowing device which signals the actual death of her lover at the front. Another parallelism which can be drawn between these two specific experiences of memory loss concerns the need to resort to photographs as memory objects in order to recapture a sharp image of the recently deceased (5, 142).[22]

Woven within the interspersed chapters of "The Blind Assassin" there is a third narrative, composed through the dialogue established by the two lovers during their furtive encounters, a socio-political dystopian parable which partly mirrors their illicit relationship.[23] The allegorical plot of this

---

22 Sharon Wilson competently argues that the photographs in *The Blind Assassin* possess the magic of magical realism and thus heighten this important dimension of the novel ("Fairy Tales, Magic Photographs" 80).

23 Magali Cornier Michael is one of the many critics who have drawn attention to the "juxtaposition of a variety of narratives" in *The Blind Assassin* (89). In "A Left-Handed Story" Karen F. Stein offers an extensive analysis of the main themes and motifs developed throughout the three interlocking novels of the same title, which are "constructed like a Russian wooden doll" (135). Hilde Staels has analyzed the mirroring devices connecting the three main narratives within the Chinese-box structure of Atwood's novel, which blends diverse

intercalated futuristic tale includes two slave children, one of whom becomes a blind assassin and the other a mute sacrificial maiden, eventually falling in love with each other. However, the love sub-plot about "the blind assassin and the tongueless girl" vanishes from the first instalment of the pulp science-fiction story which the female protagonist of the romance novel reads in a magazine while avidly searching for any publication by her absent lover that may indirectly bring her some news about him (401). Apart from a summary of the only episode which ever goes to print (399-401), what remains of the science-fiction story in *The Blind Assassin* is the oral version of a tale set in the capital-city of Planet Zycron, the site of "an ancient and once highly developed civilization" (10) and "a flourishing centre of trade and exchange" (21) whose final destruction is recurrently evoked throughout the narrative. At the beginning of the fantasy tale, the male narrator explains that he will call the city Sakiel-Norn, because its "real name [...] was erased from memory by the conquerors" so that now it is only known by the five names with which five different tribes call the "large mound of stones" built on the spot where the king and all the inhabitants of the city are supposed to be buried (11). As "each of the five tribes claims to have been the victorious attacker," all of them regard this ground as their own and continue adding stones to the heap (12). The narrator highlights his interest in the paradoxes of mnemonic phenomena by means of the following comment: "The pile of stones thus marks both an act of deliberate remembrance, and an act of deliberate forgetting" (12). This artless monument performs a task of memorialization parallel to that of the much more elaborate Port Ticonderoga's War Memorial in the sense that "these memory places function for the most part after the manner of reminders, offering in turn support for a failing memory, a struggle in the war against forgetting, even the silent plea of dead memory" (Ricoeur, *Memory* 41).

---

genres. James Harold emphasizes how "the same events are often described multiple times from different perspectives" not only in the three main narratives but also in the interspersed newspaper clippings, so that each account of the same event illuminates the others (139). Pilar Cuder has argued that the writing or telling of the futuristic science-fiction story is a collaborative literary act performed by Alex as writer or teller and Iris a reader or listener (64).

Apart from the three narratives blended in *The Blind Assassin*, there is a number of interspersed newspaper clippings which represent public memory, in juxtaposition with the private memory of the protagonist, who is responsible for having chosen such articles and who uses them either to support her account or to subvert the official version of events. This is one of the many ways in which Atwood's novel underscores questions surrounding both the nature of memory and the performance of particular acts of remembering and forgetting. Additionally, Iris resorts to various metaphors to express her thoughts about the concept of memory itself, a concept she comes to embody symbolically. Throughout her memoir, she perceives memory in succession as a mosaic constructed with fragments of the past (67), as a substance that turns people "rancid" (508), and as a requirement for revenge (508).

One of the most fascinating aspects of *The Blind Assassin* is how Iris converts "traumatic memory" into "narrative memory," to borrow Pierre Janet's terminology. Being keenly aware of the transformative potential of both memory and oblivion to heal her emotional wounds, she becomes engaged in a process of therapeutic storytelling which helps her to overcome her long-term psychological trauma.[24] She records the series of adversities she has suffered during her lifetime, including the premature death of her mother, the erratic behaviour of her seriously maimed and shell-shocked father, her everlasting and ultimately catastrophic rivalry with her mentally unstable younger sister, her miserable loveless marriage, her sad honeymoon, her ill-fated love affair, and the unfortunate destiny of her offspring. Indeed, Iris never enjoyed the pleasures of motherhood, initially due to post-natal depression and then because she was prematurely separated from her only daughter, who finished her days a victim of drug addiction. Later on, Iris was similarly deprived of the company and affection of her granddaughter, Sabrina, whose custody she also lost to her domineering sister-in-law. It is precisely to her estranged granddaughter that Iris leaves her memoir at the end of her story, shortly before her death, placing herself in Sabrina's hands as a keepsake, as a "gift" which the girl will likely refuse or might perhaps accept as her rightful "inheritance." But

---

24 While exploring *The Blind Assassin* as an example of the *Reifungsroman* genre, Rosario Arias notes that "the protagonist's life review produces a therapeutic effect in her" (7).

what is "the self" Iris is entrusting Sabrina with? The memoir makes clear that on the one hand it is Iris's *remembering self*, and on the other, an imaginative reconstruction of her former *remembered selves* which, in spite of having been obliterated by the passage of time, are paradoxically accessible now through the textual remnants to be found in the pages of her narrative.

REFERENCES

Arias Doblas, Rosario. "Moments of Ageing: The *Reifungsroman* in Contemporary Fiction." *Women Ageing Through Literature and Experience*. Ed. Brian J. Worsfold. Lleida: Universitat de Lleida, 2005. 3-12. Print.

Atwood, Margaret. "Margaret Atwood on *The Blind Assassin*." *The Guardian*. 9 Aug. 2013. Web. 9 May 2015.

---. *The Blind Assassin*. New York: Nan A. Talese, 2000. Print.

---. *Alias Grace*. London: Bloomsbury, 1996. Print.

Barzilai, Shuli. "'If You Look Long Enough': Photography, Memory and Mourning in *The Blind Assassin*." *Margaret Atwood: The Robber Bride, The Blind Assassin, Oryx and Crake*. Ed. J. Brooks Bouson. London: Continuum, 2010. 103-23. Print.

Bouson, J. Brooks. "'A Commemoration of Wounds Endured and Resented': Margaret Atwood's *The Blind Assassin* as Feminist Memoir." *Critique* 44.3 (Spring 2003): 251-69. Print.

Cooke, Natalie. "The Politics of Ventriloquism: Margaret Atwood's Fictive Confessions." *Various Atwoods*. Ed. Lorraine M. York. Toronto: Anansi, 1995. 207-28. Print.

Cuder, Pilar. "Margaret Atwood's Metafictional Acts: Collaborative Storytelling in *The Blind Assassin* and *Oryx and Crake*." *Revista Canaria de Estudios Ingleses* 56 (2008): 57-68. Print.

Dancygier, Barbara. "Narrative Anchors and the Processes of Story Construction: The Case of Margaret Atwood's *The Blind Assassin*." *Style* 41.2 (2007): 133-52. Print.

Dvorak, Marta. "The Right Hand Writing and the Left Hand Erasing in Margaret Atwood's *The Blind Assassin*." *Commonwealth Essays and Studies* 25.1 (Autumn 2002): 59-68. Print.

Gillet, Susan. "Myths of War and Peace: Margaret Atwood's *The Blind Assassin* and Ann-Marie MacDonald's *Fall on your Knees*." *eCanadian Journal of Humanities and Social Sciences* 1.1 (2012): 7-16. Print.

Harold, James. "Narrative Engagement with *Atonement* and *The Blind Assassin*." *Philosophy and Literature* 29.1 (April 2005): 130-45. Print.

Hirsch, Marianne. "The Generation of Postmemory." *Poetics Today* 29.1 (2008): 103-28. Print.

Howells, Coral Ann. "'Don't ever ask for the true story': Margaret Atwood, *Alias Grace*, and *The Blind Assassin*." *Contemporary Canadian Women's Fiction: Refiguring Identities*. New York: Palgrave, 2003. 25-52. Print.

Ingersoll, Earl G. "Waiting for the End: Closure in Margaret Atwood's *The Blind Assassin*." *Studies in the Novel* 35.4 (Winter 2003): 543-58. Print.

Janet, Pierre. *Psychological Healing: A Historical and Clinical Study*. London: Allen and Unwin, 1925. Print.

Michael, Magali Cornier. "Narrative Multiplicity and the Multi-layered Self in The *Blind Assassin*." *Margaret Atwood: The Robber Bride, The Blind Assassin, Oryx and Crake*. Ed. J. Brooks Bouson. London: Continuum, 2010. 88-102. Print.

Neisser, Ulric. "Self-Narratives: True and False." *The Remembering Self: Construction and Accuracy in the Self-Narrative*. Ed. Ulric Neisser and Robyn Fivush. Cambridge: Cambridge UP, 1994. 1-18. Print.

Parkin-Gounelas, Ruth. "'What isn't there' in Margaret Atwood's *The Blind Assassin*: The Psychoanalysis of Duplicity." *Modern Fiction Studies* 50.3 (2004): 681-700. Print.

Reed, Alison. "Disembodied Hands: Structural Duplicity in Atwood's *Blind Assassin*." *Margaret Atwood Studies* 3.1 (2009): 18-25. Print.

Renard, Virginie. *The Great War and Postmodern Memory: The First World War in Late 20th-Century British Fiction (1985-2000)*. Frankfurt am Main: Peter Lang, 2013. Print.

Ricoeur, Paul. *Memory, History, Forgetting*. Trans. Kathleen Blamey and David Pellauer. Chicago: Chicago UP, 2004. Trans. of *La Mémoire, l'histoire, l'oubli*. Paris: Seuil, 2000. Print.

---. "Reflections on a New Ethos for Europe." *Philosophy and Social Criticism* 21.5-6 (1995): 3-14. Rpt. *Paul Ricoeur: The Hermeneutics of Action*. Ed. Richard Kearney. London: SAGE, 1996. 3-13. Print.

---. *Oneself as Another*. Trans. Kathleen Blamey. Chicago: Chicago UP, 1992. Trans. of *Soi-même comme un autre*. Paris: Seuil, 1990. Print.

---. *Time and Narrative*. 3 vols. Chicago: Chicago UP, 1984-1988. Trans. of *Temps et récit*. Paris: Seuil, 1983-1985. Print.

Ridout, Alice. "'Without memory, there can be no revenge': Iris Chase Griffen's Textual Revenge in Margaret Atwood's *The Blind Assassin*." *Margaret Atwood Studies* 2.2 (December 2008): 14-25. Print.

Robinson, Alan. "*Alias Laura*: Representations of the Past in Margaret Atwood's *The Blind Assassin*." *Modern Language Review* 101.2 (April 2006): 347-59. Print.

Showalter, Elaine. "Virgin Suicide." *New Statesman*. 13.625 (2 October 2000): 53. Print.

Staels, Hilde. "Atwood's Specular Narrative: *The Blind Assassin*." *English Studies* 85.2 (April 2004): 147-60. Print.

Stein, Karen F. "Margaret Atwood's *The Blind Assassin* as a Modern 'Bluebeard.'" *21st Century Gothic: Great Gothic Novels Since 2000*. Ed. Danel Olson. Lanham: Scarecrow P, 2011. 32-41. Print.

---. "A Left-Handed Story: *The Blind Assassin*." *Margaret Atwood's Textual Assassinations: Recent Poetry and Fiction*. Ed. Sharon Rose Wilson. Columbus: Ohio State UP, 2003. 135-53. Print.

---. "Talking Back to Bluebeard: Atwood's Fictional Storytellers." *Margaret Atwood's Textual Assassinations: Recent Poetry and Fiction*. Ed. Sharon Rose Wilson. Columbus: Ohio State UP, 2003. 154-71. Print.

Strehle, Susan. *Transnational Women's Fiction: Unsettling Home and Homeland*. New York: Palgrave, 2008. Print.

Strolz, Andrea. "'True Stories' in the Course of Time in Margaret Atwood's *The Blind Assassin*." *A Sea for Encounters: Essays Towards a Postcolonial Commonwealth*. Ed. Stella Borg Barthet. Amsterdam: Rodopi, 2009. 287-306. Print.

---. *Escaping from the Prison-House of Language and Digging for Meanings in Texts Among Texts: Metafiction and Intertextuality in Margaret Atwood's Novels Lady Oracle and The Blind Assassin*. Stuttgart: Ibidem-Verlag, 2007. Print.

Schwartz, Murray. Introduction. *Memory and Desire: Aging – Literature – Psychoanalysis*. Ed. Kathleen Woodward and Murray M. Schwartz. Bloomington: Indiana UP, 1986. 1-12. Print.

Tolan, Fiona. "'Was I My Sister's Keeper?': *The Blind Assassin* and Problematic Feminisms." *Margaret Atwood: The Robber Bride, The Blind Assassin, Oryx and Crake*. Ed. J. Brooks Bouson. London: Continuum, 2010. 73-87. Print.

Watkins, Susan. "'Summoning Your Youth At Will': Memory, Time, and Aging in the Work of Penelope Lively, Margaret Atwood, and Doris Lessing." *Frontiers: A Journal of Women Studies* 34.2 (2013): 222-44. Print.

Wilson, Sharon Rose. "Fairy Tales, Magic Photographs in Atwood's *The Blind Assassin*." *Once Upon a Time: Myth, Fairy Tales and Legends in Margaret Atwood's Writings*. Ed. Sarah A. Appleton. Newcastle: Cambridge Scholars Publishing, 2008. 73-94. Print.

---. "Blindness and Survival in Margaret Atwood's Major Novels." *The Cambridge Companion to Margaret Atwood*. Ed. Coral Ann Howells. Cambridge: Cambridge UP, 2006. 176-90. Print.

"The whole aspect of age is full of possibilities!"
Traces of Ageing, Memory, and Sexuality in Daphne du Maurier's "Don't Look Now"

MARTA MIQUEL-BALDELLOU

INTRODUCTION

When Daphne du Maurier turned sixty-three years old, she published her short story "Don't Look Now," which not only tackles the issue of ageing explicitly in its plot but also becomes indicative of the influence that ageing was exerting on the later stages of her literary creativity. In her late short fiction, du Maurier presents an increasing preoccupation with identity, and in this particular story, through depicting the tragic experience of a middle-aged couple upon the sudden death of their young daughter, the author examines her own personal identity crisis in the face of ageing as well as the impact that the ageing process was having on her writing persona. The ways in which ageing affected du Maurier's literary creativity and the development of her creative voice over the years were deeply entrenched within the memories of her past and her insight into her sexuality. In fact, du Maurier went through a series of moments of personal crisis – such as the deaths of her close friend and partner Gertrude Lawrence and that of her husband Frederick Browning; moments that would come to condition her ageing process and would ultimately find their reflection in her late fiction. In the same way, the ambivalent position concerning her own sexuality that du Maurier held throughout her life – she felt, for the most part, compelled to conceal her homosexuality – also contributed to transforming her creative drive and conditioned the way she perceived the later stages of her life.

Shortly before publishing "Don't Look Now," through some of her personal letters du Maurier unveiled her ambivalent approach to ageing as she admitted that, though it had a great potential for creativity, it was also an unfathomable source of unease and dread. In a letter addressed to her good friend Oriel Malet, dated 24 January 1970, du Maurier confessed that she had considered writing a story in which a character would be incriminated once it came to light that, upon cross-examination, the subject had lied about her age. As a writer, du Maurier thus gained insight into the important role that age plays in defining one's identity and into the potential of ageing as a catalyst in the creative process; a realisation that led her to exclaim to a friend that "the whole aspect of age is full of possibilities" (*Letters from Menabilly* 240). On other occasions, du Maurier would approach age in a seemingly less positive way, as, realising that she was ageing rapidly, she increasingly began to worry about her appearance. Upon looking at some pictures of herself taken a few years before she turned sixty, du Maurier felt shocked, lamenting the fact that she believed she looked "like an old peasant woman of ninety – far older and more wrinkled than Lady Vyvyan" (*Letters from Menabilly* 194).[1] In fact, ageing was also having an impact on her sexual identity, since, as Avril Horner and Sue Zlosnik claim, in her postmenopausal stage du Maurier was afraid of "feeling asexual and potentially monstrous" (*Daphne du Maurier* 184). The highly ambivalent approach towards ageing that du Maurier displays in her personal letters would actually be transposed a few years later into her late short fiction and particularly into her short story "Don't Look Now."

---

1   When du Maurier was in her early twenties, she spent some time at Ferryside where she became acquainted with Lady Clara Vyvyan and her husband Sir Courtenay. The couple lived at Trelowarren in the Helford district which du Maurier would later describe as the most beautiful place imaginable. Lady Vyvyan was eccentric and older than the rest of du Maurier's acquaintances at the time. According to biographer Margaret Forster, Clara Vyvyan was forty-five when du Maurier, aged twenty-three, met her. From her perspective as a young girl at the time, du Maurier would always envision Lady Vyvyan as an ageing woman.

In its gothic and symbolic dimension, du Maurier's late short story "Don't Look Now" amalgamates biographical and metafictional traces that underscore echoes of her memories and of her sexuality and in this way reveals her way of approaching literary creativity in the face of old age. This article aims to analyse "Don't Look Now" examining the connections between memory, ageing, sexuality, creativity, fiction, and life. Some of the critical concepts of French philosopher Paul Ricoeur, such as the narrative quality of life, points of anchorage and emplotment, the dichotomy between memory and imagination, the notion of sameness and selfhood, and the matrix of time, remembrance, and forgetfulness will be used to pursue this aim.

PAUL RICOEUR AND NARRATIVE IDENTITY

Ricoeur refers to the "pre-narrative dimension of life" when he argues that life experience presents a virtual narrativity and can be defined as an incipient story in demand of a narrative. According to Ricoeur, narrative identity is created by means of the transformation of the data pertaining to one's life into a narrative, and this narrative composition of life then becomes instrumental in giving shape to our own identity as we ultimately construct it by telling ourselves a story of our own life. In this respect, du Maurier's short fiction emphasises the interaction between life and narrative so much so that her biographer Margaret Forster argued that du Maurier's "writing of the stories was certainly to a very great extent a kind of therapy" (300). It could be claimed that du Maurier gave shape to the narrative identity of her ageing process through the writing of her late short fiction.

In relation to the concept of narrative identity, Ricoeur also makes use of the term "points of anchorage" to refer to a chain of biographical episodes in which we are inclined to identify "stories that demand to be told" ("Life in Quest of Narrative" 30).[2] In fact, it can be argued that a

---

2   In this essay, Ricoeur mentions three different types of points of anchorage "that we find for narrative understanding in living experience." The first point of anchorage consists in our familiarity with the conceptual network of human acting and suffering which is "of the same order as our familiarity with the plots

series of incidents that occurred at the time of du Maurier's journeys to the city of Venice came to constitute a series of points of anchorage – that is, episodes in her life that possessed a potential for narrative – which unleashed the author's creativity and ultimately gave shape to the plot of her short story "Don't Look Now," whose action is set in that Italian city. Likewise, Ricoeur contends that due to the elusive character of real life we need the help of fiction to organise it in retrospect since stories are not simply an enumeration of events in serial order but are organised intelligibly. It is in this sense that Ricoeur refers to the concept of "emplotment" which consists in the synthesis of heterogeneous elements and is aimed at drawing a narrative configuration out of a succession of events (21).

Accordingly, du Maurier's short story "Don't Look Now" exemplifies the blurring of fact and fiction as it narrates events that actually took place during the course of the author's journeys to Venice, events that are mingled with incidents that arose in her literary imagination. In his writings, Ricoeur focuses on the similarities as well as the differences that can be drawn between memory and imagination. He claims that memory has been considered to function within the province of imagination; both purportedly work on the association of ideas and can easily be confused since memories also turn into images. Conversely though, only imagination is directed towards the fantastic while memories are drawn towards reality, and it is only memory, as opposed to imagination, which is associated with the past.

In the course of du Maurier's short story present occurrences whose actuality is put into question awaken mournful memories as the past becomes intertwined with the present. As we shall see, John, the protagonist of the story, is haunted by the vision of a young girl in a red pixie hood who wanders around the streets of Venice and who reminds him of his late young daughter. In this context, Ricoeur claims that although

---

of stories that are known to us." The second point of anchorage lies in "the symbolic resources of the practical field" (28) as all human experiences, like narratives, are mediated by all sorts of symbolic systems such as signs, rules, or norms. Finally, the third point of anchorage consists in "the pre-narrative quality of human experience" (29) as life is in permanent search of a narrative and it is not by chance that we commonly speak of stories that have happened to us.

traces of the past remain in our memories the past is no longer accessible to us, and it is through these memory traces that we "grasp the past again in the present" (*Memory, History, Forgetting* 436). According to Ricoeur, the memory trace should be envisioned "as a present effect and as the sign of an absent cause" (426), that is, as something that is always present in our minds and does not involve any sort of absence. In this respect, the trace exemplifies "the aporia of the presence of the absence" (10), and, as a case in point, in du Maurier's narrative the fact that John sees a young girl that reminds him of his daughter brings to the fore a trace from the past that remains enduringly present.

In the context of personal identity, Ricoeur contends that narrative identity is made up of "the dialectic of selfhood and sameness" (*Oneself as Another* 140), as the self needs both sorts of identity to constitute itself. Drawing on the distinction between *idem* and *ipse*, Ricoeur claims that the *idem*-identity or self-sameness – as opposed to the notion of difference – is immutable and remains identical over the passage of time while the *ipse*-identity or selfhood has a problematic relation with permanence in time since human experience negates the concept of immutability as nothing really eludes change in the experience of the self. In fact, to use Ricoeur's words, "the concept of narrative identity offers a solution to the aporias of personal identity" ("Narrative Identity" 192) as it paves the way for the dialogue between sameness and selfhood that conforms personal identity. In this sense, narrative identity acts as "a mediator between the pole of character (where *idem* and *ipse* tend to coincide) and the pole of self-maintenance (where selfhood frees itself from sameness)" (*Oneself as Another* 118-19). In "Don't Look Now," du Maurier delineated the evolution of her writing persona as she stood on the threshold of old age through the overlaps and gaps between the *idem* and the *ipse* of her creative voice. John, the character on whom the narrative focuses, faces the dialectic between his same and his self, having suffered a tragic experience that had a disruptive effect on his personal identity.

In relation to time, Ricoeur refers to Aristotle to underline "the value of narrative for putting our temporal existence into order" ("Life in Quest of Narrative" 31). The philosopher describes the "discordant concordance" that characterises narrative in contrast with the "concordant discordance" that characterises time (32), that is, a narrative underlines the connections that unify multiple actions over a span of time. In "Don't Look Now," characters move between memories and premonitions that condition their present existence: One of the ageing female twins the married couple encounters is able to read their tragic past while John – the protagonist of the story – exemplifies a case of narrative prolepsis as he has the vision of a future event that has not yet taken place. Nonetheless, in spite of this "concordant discordance" in terms of time, the narration of all the events throughout the story acquires a "discordant concordance" owing to its narrative quality. In other words, narratives draw together disparate and discordant elements into the unity and concordance of a plot.

For Ricoeur, memory can be defined as a struggle against forgetting while forgetting is experienced as an attack on the reliability of memory. He distinguishes, however, between the idea of "definitive forgetting" which consists of the total erasing of memory traces and the idea of "reversible forgetting" which is positive, remains latent, and is considered the reverse of forgetting (*Memory, History, Forgetting* 414). In du Maurier's short story, John, as opposed to his wife Laura, tries to repress the painful memories of the death of his daughter only to gain insight into the fact that he finds himself caught in a latent forgetting as these repressed memories are just about to emerge. Likewise, from her own perspective by giving shape to a short story with significant biographical and metafictional echoes, du Maurier also resorted to the reserve of forgetting, as a series of personal memories awakened through the process of literary creation.

In the course of remembering, Ricoeur also makes use of philosopher Edward Casey's series of mnemonic modes such as reminding, reminiscing, and recognising (36) which point at different ways in which memories are brought to mind. The act of reminding involves recalling from the past by means of clues that guard against forgetting and are found in the form of external points of reference; the mnemonic mode of reminiscing consists in awakening the past through collective evocation; the act of recognising makes acknowledgement possible and enables us to know in the present what comes from the past so that it becomes possible to reintroduce into the present what appeared to have been forgotten and so erased from memory. As we shall see, in du Maurier's short story, John and, by extension, du Maurier herself, experiences different instances of these mnemonic modes. As the past impinges on the present it is brought to new life through collective evocation so that what seemed to have been forgotten is reintroduced again into the present.

THE NARRATIVE QUALITY OF LIFE, POINTS OF ANCHORAGE, AND EMPLOTMENT

Even though some of du Maurier's short stories had already been published individually in different periodicals during her youth, she first published a collection of short fiction when she was over forty-five, and she continued to do so up to the end of her life, writing the bulk of her short pieces at a later stage of creativity. Unlike her gothic romances with Victorian hues that gave her worldwide fame, du Maurier's short fiction is characterised, to use Horner and Zlosnik's words, "by a fascination with the macabre and sinister, by irruptions of the irrational, and by a knack of presenting the chill of the unfamiliar within the familiar" ("Glimpses of the Dark Side" 242). Her short stories often attain a significantly darker, psychological, and more introspective tone with veiled references to biographical episodes which underscore events that had a deep effect on her life both personally and creatively. In her biography of du Maurier, Margaret Foster claims that the tension in many of du Maurier's stories originated in a series of distressing emotional experiences that she had to endure at the time such as problems in her marital life, the guilt of infidelity, the acceptance of her homosexuality, and the death of her loved ones.

Taking into consideration the blending of life with fiction in du Maurier's short fiction, her late short story "Don't Look Now" can be taken as illustrative of Ricoeur's theories about the narrative quality of life. The narrative composition of life plays a role in the fashioning of our identity since according to Ricoeur, "the story of a life grows out of stories that have not been recounted and that have been repressed in the direction of actual stories which the subject could take charge of and consider to be constitutive of his personal identity" ("Life in Quest of Narrative" 30). In the writing of "Don't Look Now," du Maurier seemed to find in her lived experience a virtual sort of narrativity. By means of transforming different incidents of her own life into a unified narrative and by constructing a story about somebody else based on events that happened to her, through a process of emplotment du Maurier gave shape to her narrative identity, making sense of her identity as an individual as well as a writer at this later stage of creativity.

The plot of du Maurier's short story "Don't Look Now" revolves around a married couple, John and Laura, who spend their holidays in

Venice to attempt to recover from the recent and tragic loss of their young daughter Christine. Their aim of forgetting the past is soon jeopardised when they meet two old female twins, one of whom has psychic powers, who not only claim they have visions of the deceased girl but also assert that Christine is sending her parents a message of warning, declaring that they run a terrible risk should they remain in Venice. From her middle-age onwards, du Maurier made several journeys to Venice which would subsequently evoke memories of a series of turning points in her life. It can be argued that this life experience presented a virtual narrativity for the author that would ultimately find its reflection in fiction. Likewise, a chain of personal episodes in the author's life with a potential for narrative, a series of points of anchorage, are fictionalised through the process of emplotment and are present throughout this short story.

The fact that du Maurier made two trips to Venice at different critical junctures in her life sheds light upon the significance that the author would subsequently attach to this Italian city. Du Maurier made her first trip there when she was forty-five shortly after the death of her much-loved friend and partner, the actress Gertrude Lawrence.[3] On this first trip to Venice, du Maurier and her husband Frederick Browning were invited to join Ronald Armstrong with whom they had become acquainted after he had declared his fervent admiration for du Maurier in a letter. However, since her husband had hurt his arm, only du Maurier travelled to Venice to join her pen friend, a homosexual considerably older than she and with whom she would soon become quite intimate. Thirteen years later, du Maurier travelled to Venice for a second time; she was then fifty-eight and again in mourning for the death of a loved one, her husband who had recently passed away. It was an intensely traumatic time for the author who felt nostalgia and guilt in equal degrees upon reflecting on the years of her marriage which had been haunted by the spectre of suspicion and infidelity on the part of both her husband and herself. Her emotional turmoil at the

---

3 According to Margaret Forster, du Maurier often equated the loss of her friend Gertrude Lawrence with the loss of her own father since both of them had symbolised for the author a sort of Peter Pan spirit she thought would never really allow them to grow old. Gertrude's death ultimately made du Maurier reflect on the inexorability of time and, by extension, on her own process of ageing (266).

time had a huge impact on her writing and du Maurier envisioned her second visit to Venice as an attempt to regain her creative drive which she thought she had utterly lost after her husband's death. According to Forster, du Maurier then addressed a letter to her editor, Victor Gollancz, in which she stated that her imagination was completely fallow as a result of her emotional shock and that she was afraid that this experience "had dried her imagination up for good." Du Maurier considered the possibility of "trying a holiday in the hope of stimulating" her barren imagination, ultimately choosing Venice as her destination (351).

Issues such as du Maurier's anxiety about her losing her capacity to write, her ambivalent memories of her marriage, and the inherent presence of death contributed to a sense of gloom that pervaded her writing at the time. "Don't Look Now" elaborates on many of these points of anchorage in her life. As the plot unfolds, it is revealed that John and Laura first travelled to Venice during their honeymoon and that this is not their first but actually their third visit to Venice in the course of their marriage. The setting of the story acquires a symbolic meaning for the characters since Venice has borne witness to the evolution of their relationship from the first days of marriage to the present tragic time. As an analogy with du Maurier's ambivalent feelings towards her marriage, the plot also focuses on the lack of communication and understanding between the couple who deal with Christine's death very differently: John avoids talking about it and Laura often brings up the topic in their conversations. The sense of loss and despair is symbolised by the labyrinthine streets of Venice that John and Laura continually walk through and around which they frequently end up losing their way despite their familiarity with the city. Ultimately, this convoluted and intricate scenario reflects the emotional turmoil that both characters undergo. As Forster claims, it is also evocative of the sense of trauma and disorientation that du Maurier went through at the time. The underlying and endemic presence of death seems to permeate the whole of the story especially when they learn that the police are investigating a series of murders that have been taking place in the city.

Sexuality also reveals itself as a lurking presence in the story as it is in Venice that John and Laura have their first sexual encounter after weeks of unbearable strain following their daughter's demise. Any happy memories of the days of their honeymoon and of their first intimacy remain in sharp contrast to the tension and lack of complicity that begin to set in between husband and wife at the time. Du Maurier had in mind her own marriage as a point of anchorage to depict the tension resulting from the marital problems that affect the couple in the story. Nonetheless, references to sexuality in the narrative go beyond the sexual encounter of the married couple, as there are significant, though covert, allusions to homosexual intercourse which inevitably bring to mind du Maurier's own homosexuality. In fact, as Forster points out, du Maurier often made use of the word "Venetian" as a code word for "lesbian" (28) and claimed that she had "Venetian tendencies" to refer to her homosexual inclinations, given the affairs she had with women, such as her platonic love for Ellen Doubleday, wife of her American editor, as well as the physical attraction she felt towards her long-time friend Gertrude Lawrence. At the time she wrote this short story, du Maurier also resorted to the memories of her first visit to Venice in the company of her homosexual friend Ronald Armstrong. It can be argued that this short story metaphorically becomes part of the author's narrative identity thereby acquiring a symbolic meaning as du Maurier identified the virtual narrativity of this series of biographical events that would ultimately be transposed in her fiction and would give shape to her narrative identity.

Through the process of writing her short story, du Maurier also came to terms with her sexual identity both as a woman in a heterosexual marriage as well as a woman with a homosexual identity. However, given her Victorian upbringing, du Maurier found sexuality in her married life respectable while she always felt hesitant, or even reluctant, to give vent to her homosexuality. As Forster claims, du Maurier never wanted to be "Venetian" and even felt frightened to admit to herself that she had any "Venetian tendencies" at all, especially since she was brought up in the knowledge of her father's homophobic attitudes (28). And yet, ever since she was young, du Maurier was well aware of a 'male' sexual identity living within her – "the boy in the box" – that was mainly responsible for fuelling her literary creativity (Forster 276). She would inextricably link her sexual drive to her creative force. In "Don't Look Now" there are veiled references to homosexuality that underline du Maurier's ambivalent position with regard to her own homosexual identity. After their first meeting the two ageing female twins, John and Laura give vent to their imagination and indulge in a guessing game to find out what the twins might be doing in Venice. The married couple imagines that the twins might actually be transvestites travelling around the world who have decided to liberate themselves sexually. Given their own inherent dual identity as twins, from the beginning of the story this couple of ageing women is portrayed ambivalently. On the one hand, their presence allows John and Laura to give free rein to their imaginations and leave behind, even if only momentarily, the stress and tension arising from the terrible loss they have had. On the other hand, John begins to develop a perplexing discomfort with them after having discussed that their sexual orientation might be lesbianism. The vacillating perception of the ageing female twins that the married couple has – especially Laura as she grows fascinated by them, while John bluntly shows his anxiety – goes hand-in-hand with du Maurier's dual views of her own sexual identity.

This ambivalent interpretation of homosexuality in the short story as displayed through its main characters also extends to du Maurier's dual views on ageing. In spite of the married couple's initial contemptuous opinion about them, the ageing female twins actually prove to be more able as well as wiser in their own guessing game since one of them, as a result of her psychic powers, actually manages to gain insight into the tragedy that John and Laura are going through. However, du Maurier's short story also underscores anxiety about the aged female body insofar as it unleashes the ghost of masculinisation in the way it is presented in the story and, by extension, refers back to du Maurier's early identification of a 'male' identity in her persona, that is, "the boy she explained she had 'locked up in a box' long ago" in her youth (Forster 221). Significantly, John's description of one of the ageing female twins depicts her look as remarkably masculine:

> She would be in her middle sixties, he supposed, the masculine shirt with collar and tie, sports jacket, grey tweed coming to mid-calf. Grey stockings and laced black shoes. He had seen the type on golf-courses and at dog-shows – invariably showing not sporting breeds but pugs – and if you came across them at a party in somebody's house they were quicker on the draw with a cigarette-lighter than he was himself, a mere male, with pocket-matches. (9)

John's masculinised perception of the ageing twins, as well as his discomfort and even hatred during their causal meetings with them on the streets of Venice, ultimately inform on du Maurier's own uneasiness about sexuality and old age. By means of the narrative's focus on the character of John, according to Ella Westland, du Maurier's short story also underscores "a sense of repulsion at the idea of physically unattractive older women having sex at all" (139), thus implying that, from John's patriarchal and even ageist view, aged women can become a source of contempt.

The description of the twins at the beginning of the story foretells the abrupt final appearance of an eminently dual character, an androgynous ageing dwarf, whose presence remains present but not visible throughout the narrative but whose identity is not revealed until the very end. The eventual revelation of her identity gives the story circularity due to her ambiguous nature – John persistently mistakes her for somebody else –, reminiscent of the twins who make their appearance at the onset of the story. The conclusion that this short story reaches through the final revelation of this unexpected "other" gives shape to du Maurier's ambivalent identity in terms of her sexuality and her process of ageing as well as how both conditioned her literary creativity.

MEMORY, IMAGINATION, AND CREATIVITY

The constant interaction between her own life and narrativity that pervades du Maurier's story and underlines the notion of the narrative quality of life also emphasises Ricoeur's focus on the comparative analysis between memory and imagination, as memories of past incidents also imbue fictionalised events in du Maurier's narrative. As seen above, both recalling and imagining operate on the association of ideas and are tied by contiguity so "to evoke one – to imagine it – is to evoke the other – to remember it" (*Memory, History, Forgetting* 5). In this respect, du Maurier's short story "Don't Look Now" is a piece of fiction and, so, of imagination that to a great extent relies on the author's memories of her personal experiences.

The story is also endowed with an important metafictional quality that includes direct references to du Maurier's creative process as a writer. As Forster reveals, du Maurier often made use of the phrase that gives the title to this narrative – 'don't look now' – whenever she felt like "launching into an entertaining fantasy about someone she was observing" (376). This happens at the opening of this narrative when John and Laura draw on the same phrase when they start making guesses about the twins who are sitting at a table nearby:

"Don't look now," John said to his wife, "but there are a couple of old girls two tables away who are trying to hypnotise me." [...] "They're not old girls at all," she said. "They're male twins in drag." [...] Pretend to choke," he said, "then they won't notice. You know what it is – they're criminals doing the sights of Europe, changing sex at each stop. Twin sisters here on Torcello. Twin brothers tomorrow in Venice, or even tonight, parading arm-in-arm across the Piazza San Marco. Just a matter of switching clothes and wigs." (7)

For du Maurier, the common use of the phrase that gives this story its title refers to the occasions on which the author indulged in creativity. It became a cue that awakened memories of former creative moments as well as a marker that she commonly used to unleash her imagination and cross the threshold into fiction. The interaction between imagination and memory at work within her process of creativity is reflected as the guessing game that John and Laura play turns into a memory of the happy years of their marriage when they used to make up stories about the strangers they met. Nonetheless, by using this phrase the couple also mark the beginning of a narrative in which they will transform themselves from mere narrators into the main characters of their own fantasies as they, in turn, become the focus of attention of the twins they have been fantasising about. Their guessing game contrasts with one of the ageing twins' psychic visions as the happy memories of their past are offset by the twins' vision of John and Laura's late daughter which reawakens sad memories about their recent terrible loss.

    The author's personal circumstances that gave rise to the story shed light on the story's coupling of memories and imagination along with its important metafictional content. The last journey that du Maurier made to Venice, this time in the company of her younger sister Jeanne, was intended as an attempt to stimulate her imagination in a period of acute emotional upheaval. Years later some of the memories she had from this journey would lay the groundwork for her story "Don't Look Now." As Forster claims, du Maurier's fictional psychic twins were based on an actual pair of elderly twins that had caught the author's attention when she visited Torcello. In the course of her visit to Venice, du Maurier was shocked at the sight of a young girl that ultimately turned out to be a woman dwarf (376). This real episode in du Maurier's life would give shape to one of the leitmotifs of her short story since John keeps on seeing what he believes to be a girl in a pixie hood who reminds him of his late daughter and whom he desperately seeks to protect. Her real identity as a woman dwarf is dramatically revealed at the end.

Du Maurier's memories of the twin sisters and the dwarf can be identified as memory traces engraved on her short story. Drawing on Ricoeur's definition, a memory trace is defined as "an affection resulting from the shock of an event that can be said to be striking" (*Memory, History, Forgetting* 14) as if it was an imprint preserved in a block of wax after having pressed a stamp on it. The initial affection that the real vision of the twins and the dwarf produced on du Maurier definitely left a trace in her memory which prevailed over time and whose effect reverberated in spite of the absence of its original cause. This initial affection surprised and astonished du Maurier and, in her late years, the author appeared to make use of it to form the basis of her story.

Du Maurier's intermingling of memories and fiction is also exemplified by the significance that the city of Venice acquires as the plot unfolds. The author had visited Venice before and had significant memories of it, but she also seemed to resort to the fact that over time it had acquired a plethora of literary connotations within the collective literary imagination. With echoes of Thomas Mann's novella *Death in Venice* (*Der Tod in Venedig*, 1912),[4] the setting of du Maurier's short story also becomes a symbolic site with connotations of death and decay as John and Laura try to overcome the loss of their daughter while a series of murders puts the safety and wellbeing of tourists and citizens at risk. Despite the fact that Venice is a holiday resort – since John and Laura chose it as the destination for their honeymoon – it is also endowed with a dark underside as depicted by its mess of convoluted canals that give shape to a virtual labyrinth. This maze of canals and passages brings to mind the dormant presence of some organic being, of a body, which underlines the importance that physicality and sexuality acquire in the story, also in clear analogy with Thomas Mann's *Death in*

---

4   It should also be noted that Luchino Visconti's classic adaptation of Thomas Mann's original novella to the cinema was released in 1971, the year that du Maurier's short story "Don't Look Now" was published.

Venice. Du Maurier also makes use of the fact that the Venice has traditionally been associated with carnival – as Edgar Allan Poe's seminal tale "The Cask of Amontillado" demonstrates – evoking its association with the world of masquerade. John and Laura imagine that the twins are actually male transvestites while an ageing female dwarf dresses as a child in a pixie hood. This fascination with masquerade and disguise ultimately connotes a play of identities which is evocative of du Maurier's ambiguous selves in terms of her sexual identity and her process of ageing and how they affected her creativity.

In the course of time and also of her creative process, du Maurier would endow the initial inscription of her memories with a sense of estrangement and with the symbolic personification of the figure of "the other." The sense of unease and disquiet, embodied in the story by the mysterious ageing twins as well as the dwarf underpins the author's ambivalent views on her process of ageing, her sexuality, and her literary creativity at a later stage. Du Maurier's memories of a dwarf she saw during one of her visits to Venice already contained the potential for ambiguity in its initial affection, since the author herself, like John in the story, mistook a dwarf for a child. The author turned this real character she kept in her memory into a fictional archetype of otherness whose symbolic nature enabled her to display her fears of old age.

There is more than meets the eye in the initial sense of estrangement that John and Laura feel towards the twins as well as in the increasing curiosity that John shows towards an apparently young girl in a pixie hood. At the onset of the story, to the astonishment of the married couple, the two aged twins give evidence that they know about the death of young Christine and, in the final scene of the story, John notices that the young girl he has been trying to protect ultimately removes her pixie hood and becomes a deadly aged woman dwarf, turning from an apparently innocent victim into a literal murderess. These epiphanic scenes which mark the beginning and the end of the story also acquire a symbolic meaning from the perspective of ageing which is symptomatic of the author's ambivalence towards her own becoming older. John and Laura adopt an ambiguous approach towards the ageing female twins they meet since at first the twins are a source of scorn and amusement, but soon Laura grows fascinated by them and John anxious. The ongoing presence of the ageing twins forces the married couple to face their suppressed fears and verbalise their contained suffering as a result of their daughter's recent death.

It can be argued that the twins become ageing doubles of the protagonists of the story inasmuch as there is a sort of mirror effect created, as John and Laura exchange glances with them. Significantly, Laura makes use of a pocket mirror to catch a better glimpse of the ageing twins: "Laura took the powder compact from her bag and held it in front of her face, the mirror acting as a reflector" (8). This sense of duality also extends to the double effect created between the couple's daughter, Christine, and the ageing dwarf that John encounters in the streets of Venice, since John identifies the dwarf with his late daughter when he first mistakes the dwarf for a little girl. The dwarf defies any attempt at defining identity as she moves through the middle ground between youth and old age, maleness and femaleness, as well as hope and death. Du Maurier's creation of this grotesque character in her late short fiction underscores her ambivalent feelings about the process of ageing at the time which would have a twofold effect on her literary creativity.

THE WRITING PERSONA AND THE CRISIS OF IDENTITY

Du Maurier's "Don't Look Now" underscores the author's understanding and process of coming to terms with the evolution of her writing persona, and this becomes noticeable in the story by means of its remarkable metafictional undertones which lay bare some of the author's creative mechanisms and the way in which she approached this later stage of creativity. As Ella Westland mentions, du Maurier's short story unfolds mostly through the perspective of a male character with "a controlling voice" (137) who ultimately reveals his vulnerability and meets his demise as the story comes to a close. Bearing in mind that in her letters and autobiographical writings du Maurier often referred to her creative voice as essentially 'male,' there is a concealed identification of the author's writing persona with the main character, John. Drawing on this identification and the tragic end that awaits John, critics such as Horner and Zlosnik have claimed that the story anticipates "the death of the author's writing persona" ("Glimpses of the Dark Side" 248). At the age of sixty-three, the fear of loss of mental creativity and age led du Maurier to write an elegy to her 'male' creative voice, which would ultimately pave the way for the subsequent transformation of her writing persona at this later stage of creativity.

According to Forster, when du Maurier was in her forties, she grew attracted to Carl Jung's philosophical precepts, particularly to his idea that each person has dual aspects within a single self (276). In a letter to her daughter Flavia, du Maurier disclosed that "she had always been able to feel within herself two quite separate personalities," – male and female –, arguing that the one that was "madly boyish" (qtd. in Forster 276) was mostly in charge when she was writing. Du Maurier also unveiled that she had to live with the existence of these two distinct selves and often felt it was particularly difficult to control her 'male' persona. Even though she admitted that her 'male' personality often caused her trouble, she confessed that it was also the one that usually fuelled her creativity and that without it her writing would have been virtually non-existent. Du Maurier conceived her writing as a way to release the thoughts and ideas that disturbed her, but, in particular, she envisioned her creativity as an attempt to exorcise what she perceived to be a great fear of reality. Accordingly, to use Forster's words, when du Maurier's ability to create began to decrease as she aged, the author could not help equating the death of the writer with "the death of the self" (419).

Du Maurier went on to admit that she gained insight into the full meaning of death when her husband passed away. In fact, she claimed that "this encounter with reality can so awaken the writer from the imaginary world that *he* never recovers" ("Death and Widowhood" 122-23). Even though Du Maurier's use of the male pronoun 'he' may simply respond to the generic gender-neutral third-person pronoun for the time she was writing in, it is still noticeable that she makes use of the male pronoun to refer to herself as a writer in this case, especially noticing that, in other parts of the same text, she explicitly refers to the figure of the writer using the male and female pronouns, stating that "it is when death touches the writer in real life that he, or she, realises the full impact of its meaning" ("Death and Widowhood" 122). She was drawn into the harsh reality of her everyday life and found it hard to go back to writing. She interpreted the emotional shock after her husband's death as a turning point that began to mark the decline of her writing persona. In this respect, a significantly elegiac tone pervades "Don't Look Now" inasmuch as the story unfolds from John's perspective as he struggles to leave behind the tragic loss of his daughter but finds himself unable to do so. As opposed to his wife, John believes he is in control of the circumstances, but he literally becomes a victim of them as he gradually finds himself caught in an emotional crisis. John is reluctant to remember, and he tries to repress the painful memories of his past although their symbolic return will ultimately be lethal.

In an essay she wrote in 1966, when she was on the point of turning sixty, du Maurier reflected on death in her writings and in her personal life. To use her own words, "death, to the novelist, is a familiar theme" ("Death and Widowhood" 122). Upon equating the figure of the author with that of a successful murderess, she acknowledged her authority as a writer over all her characters in the following way:

> I can even confess I enjoyed the killing. It gave a certain zest to the writing, and if I felt an inward pang for the loss of the character I had created, the pang was soon forgotten and the memory faded. The fictitious person was, after all, only a puppet of my imagination, and I could create others to take his place. The writer, like a spider, spins a web; the creatures caught in the web have no substance, no reality. (122)

Nonetheless, this confidence gradually diminished with the advent of her own ageing, when du Maurier began to identify with a transitional self that intermittently switched roles from a confident murderess in her fiction to a frightened victim. In fact, in spite of his initial confidence, not only does John have an emotional crisis but he also dies at the hands of a grotesque ageing murderess – du Maurier's *alter ego*, judging from her words in her autobiographical writing. Du Maurier's fiction at the time can be described as symptomatic of a personal crisis but also of the potential for the transformation of her writing persona. Ricoeur's concept of narrative identity becomes a tool with which to shed light on this matter. The dialectic between same and self, which is entangled in the concept of identity, is explored through narrative mediation and contributes to the individual's interpretation of his or her self, ultimately fulfilling the Aristotelian purgative and cathartic function of literature. Du Maurier's pursuit of her narrative identity and the development of her writing persona as reflected in her story as the crisis of the characters' identity is problematised through the dialectic between the same and the self.

Even if John and Laura still remain together and travel to the same city they visited on their honeymoon, clinging to the hope they will be able to stick to their old selves, a significant change has taken place and they realise fact that nothing will ever be the same. To use Ricoeur's terms, the scission between the same and the self that they exemplify unveils their identity crisis which is echoed throughout the narrative. John and Laura find themselves back in Venice years after their first visit, and, even though they are the same individuals, their selves are no longer the same. There is a split between their *idem*-identity and their *ipse*-identity, as selfhood begins to detach itself from sameness. This sense of crisis is symbolised through different narratological elements that endow the story with a significant postmodern quality, such as the prevalence of an unreliable character through which the story is mainly canalised, the disquiet arising from mistaken identities, the use of metafiction to lay bare the intricacies of the process of fictionalisation, the subversion of time frameworks, and the presence of an intimidating setting.

The sense of crisis that prevails in the story betrays a less confident authorial voice as John is used to echo du Maurier's literary voice. John appears to be unreliable as a character since for most of the story he is mistaken about the real identity of the young girl in the pixie hood. Even though most of the narrative is from John's perspective, his unexpected death at the end of the narrative ultimately suggests that the story is eerily focused on a ghost. The story is endowed with significant metafictional undertones as John himself gives closure to the narrative exclaiming "what a bloody silly way to die" (55) as if he was commenting on an unexpected twist of the plot that he, as a character, considered to be too far-fetched. Time frameworks are also subverted as John feels himself caught between memories that he tries to repress and a totally unknown personal gift that allows him to have premonitions. It is not only the past but also the future that impinges on the present in the temporal configuration of the story.

A sense of personal crisis is also reflected in the physical setting since John and Laura walk along the streets of Venice and often fall prey to a haunting and overwhelming sensation of loss and dislocation which is symptomatic of their psychological condition and also of the reserve and detachment that begin to characterise their marriage. This sense of crisis is brought to the fore through the description of the labyrinthine streets of Venice:

The canal was narrow, the houses on either side seemed to close in upon it, and in the daytime, with the sun's reflection on the water and the windows of the houses open, bedding upon the balconies, a canary singing in a cage, there had been an impression of warmth, of secluded shelter. Now, ill-lit, almost in darkness, the windows of the houses shuttered, the water dank, the scene appeared altogether different, neglected, poor, and the long narrow boats moored to the slippery steps of cellar entrances looked like coffins. (19)

This pervasive sense of doom and death reflects the couple's miserable condition following the death of their daughter, but it also foretells the tragic end that awaits John. It can be argued that this sense of loss is also evocative of du Maurier's own crisis of authorial identity, given the parallelisms that can be established between John and the author's creative voice. His death at the end of the story echoes the author's decline of creativity but also prepares for the transformation of her writing persona.

THE NOTION OF TIME, REMEMBERING, AND FORGETTING

According to Richard Kelly, du Maurier gradually grew aware of "the ghosts of her past that continued to develop over the years" (8) as she found out that her past often re-emerged in her present. In her autobiography *Growing Pains*, which she wrote at the age of seventy, du Maurier claimed that "we are none of us isolated in time, but we are part of what we were once, and of what we are yet to become so that these varied personalities merge and become one in creative thought" (65). She resorted to the blurring of timeframes in the composition of her story "Don't Look Now" which, in turn, echoed her reflections on her present situation as an author, as she blended the memories of her past and the expectations of her future to write an elegy about her writing persona. Once again, drawing on Ricoeur's terms, du Maurier was aware of the "concordant discordance of time" that transforms into the "discordant concordance of narrative." To make sense of disparate elements that gave shape to reality, she endowed them with an orderly narrative configuration which would ultimately form her narrative identity.

In du Maurier's story, memories and premonitions overlap and bring to the fore a sense of dislocation that becomes symptomatic of the identity crisis befalling the protagonist. In the story the twin sister that is endowed with psychic powers sets off the married couple's emotional crisis as she tells them about the death of their daughter. In spite of John's blatant scepticism, this twin sister discloses that John also possesses a psychic gift that allows him to see the future. In fact, John has a vision of an event, Laura's coming back to Venice after having left Italy for England on account of their son's sudden illness, that has not taken place yet and mistakes it for a present occurrence. Nonetheless, John is totally unaware of the fact that he has had a premonition of what is yet to come. This event acquires further importance when, in a display of dramatic irony, it is revealed that Laura goes back to Venice in the future because she has been informed about her husband's death while John in spite of his premonition remains ignorant of the tragic fate that awaits him.

"Don't Look Now" also explores the dilemma between remembering and forgetting. While Laura clings to her past, John clings to the present. To use Ricoeur's categorisation of forgetting, in the story John would exemplify "latent forgetting" or "forgetting kept in reverse" as opposed to the "definitive forgetting" or the erasing of traces to which he initially aspires. Nonetheless, in spite of his reluctance to remember, John goes through a process of different mnemonic modes that, according to Ricoeur, amount to reminding, reminiscing, recognising, and ultimately surrendering to recollection. The twins who speak to the couple about the presence of their late daughter unleash a process of "reminiscence" as they collectively force the couple to address the issue. John appears to come to terms with his past as he reintroduces it into the present by what he believes to be a process of "recognition" of the girl in a pixie hood who will ultimately become the personification of "the other" in the context of remembrance. According to Ricoeur, that which is recognised in the process of remembering is recognised as doubly "other" inasmuch as "it is absent (other than presence) and it is earlier (other than present)" (*Memory, History, Forgetting* 36). In this sense, the first time that John lays eyes on the girl, she clearly awakens some memories he does not even dare to admit to himself. He is relieved when he realises that his wife has not even noticed her. John's acknowledged relief betrays the fact that the girl has inevitably "reminded" him of his late daughter and assumes that this event would have equally awakened distressing memories in his wife if had she seen the girl. From then on, John's dormant memories are slowly awakened, as he misidentifies his daughter as the girl that wanders the streets of Venice. When he discovers the actual subject hiding behind its innocent appearance, John gains insight into his fatal mistake. In an epiphanic scene, John witnesses the uncanny transformation that the girl undergoes, as she turns into a fearsome epitome of otherness:

The child struggled to her feet and stood before him, the pixie-hood falling from her head on to the floor. He stared at her, incredulity turning to horror, to fear. It was not a child at all but a little thick-set woman dwarf, about three feet high, with a great square adult head too big for her body, grey locks hanging shoulder-length, and she wasn't sobbing any more, she was grinning at him, nodding her head up and down. (55)

In this scene, John finds out that the helpless child that reminded him of his daughter is actually an adult dwarf, guilty of having committed a series of murders in the city of Venice. John pays too high a price for his mistaken perception; although he manages to ascertain the actual identity of a murderess, but, in so doing, he also meets his own death. His reluctance to remember ultimately meets an uncanny end since as he stares the dwarf in the eye – the embodiment of the abject –, he is also compelled to face what he most dreads: the painful memories of the past, the advent of ageing, and the inevitability of death. The dwarf personifies his deepest fears, which, after being repressed, ultimately make their appearance in a violent and disruptive manner. Unlike his wife, John refuses to believe, despite the twins's admonitions, that their late daughter is trying to warn them. As the story ends, the dwarf "fumbled in her sleeve, drawing a knife, and as she threw it at him with hideous strength, piercing his throat, he stumbled and fell" (55). According to Horner and Zlosnik, the final scene of the story in which John confronts the transformation of the girl into an androgynous dwarf with a phallic knife can be symbolically interpreted as John's "fear of castration" (*Daphne du Maurier* 176), his fears of emasculation and powerlessness after his loss.

In a biographical interpretation, John's death and the dwarf in the story symbolise du Maurier's fears of ageing and her concern about the decline of her creative drive. In the last years of her life, du Maurier began to lose her memory and her capacity to distinguish fiction from actual fact. In this context, as Ricoeur asserts, fiction has "a role to play in the apprenticeship of dying," since narratives serve the purpose of softening the anxiety "in the face of the unknown" (*Oneself as Another* 162). Even if John – the embodiment of du Maurier's 'male' creative drive – ultimately meets his death in the story, it can be argued that the dwarf appears to take control of du Maurier's former 'male' creative drive to transform it in her later stage of creativity. In spite of her fears, she would continue writing well into old age, proving that her age would eventually be a significantly fruitful period of creativity.

CONCLUSIONS

Taking into consideration the symbolic dimension of its final scene, du Maurier's short story "Don't Look Now" acquires significant autobiographical undertones. The ageing dwarf personifies the author's ambivalent approach towards ageing, sexuality, and creativity at that stage of her life. The dwarf speaks to the author's concern about her process of ageing – as the young girl in John's imagination transmutes into an old woman – and yet it can also be interpreted as the figure who puts an end to the author's 'male' creative drive and transforms her creative voice during her later stage of creativity. The fact that John witnesses the innocent girl's transformation into a dwarf with a phallic weapon echoes du Maurier's fearful and hesitant insight into her homosexuality during her marriage. This scene can also have an alternative interpretation where John – du Maurier's 'male' *alter ego* and, by extension, her homosexual identity – is banished by the appearance of an ageing woman who certifies du Maurier's declining sex drive in old age. Du Maurier's sexual desire always appeared to be inextricably related to her creativity inasmuch as, in her youth she devised a 'male' persona for herself whom she believed had to be suppressed according to prevailing traditional gender rules but which was nevertheless responsible for fueling her creativity. In "Don't Look Now," the male character on which the story focuses is killed by an older female who embodies du Maurier's fears of the effects that old age would have on her writing. The ageing woman of the story also personifies a powerful – no matter how old – creative drive that would allow du Maurier to keep on writing until the very last years of her life.

At the age of sixty-three, du Maurier wrote an elegy to her 'male' writing persona in the belief that her narrative voice was undergoing an unfavourable change; she found it hard to accept her ageing both as an individual and as a writer. Du Maurier appeared to exemplify what Simone de Beauvoir claimed in *The Coming of Age* that it is common for ageing people to have a distorted view of their body, ultimately seeing themselves as threatening and even grotesque. If du Maurier had admitted enjoying the killing of some of her characters, at that stage she felt that her characters could also take revenge on their creator as vengeance. As the dwarf banishes John from the story, du Maurier dramatised the decline of her writing persona through the personification of her creative voice in the character of John.

Despite du Maurier's concern about the decline of her creative drive, the truth is that it underwent a change and transformed into a more psychological and introspective voice. Her exploration of the death of the writing persona intermingles with her identification with the duplicitous presence of the ageing murderess, both portrayed as a victim and as an avenger. Du Maurier's short story can be interpreted as an attempt to exorcise her fears as an ageing writer which are fictionally canalised through the metaphorical death of her writing persona, but it can also be read as the birth of a different creative voice. This narrative exemplifies Kathleen Woodward and Murray Schwartz's conclusion that, as we age, we become what we once desired, even if this recognition may also entail an acceptance of loss (3). Having been haunted by the ghosts of her past, in her older years du Maurier was afraid of the definitive erasure of the points of anchorage in her life that had cemented her creative drive since memory ultimately involves the support of personal identity (Ricoeur, *Time and Narrative II* 12). In this sense, it could be argued that du Maurier's "boy in the box" gradually began to let the ties with the past loose. However, through the fear of forgetting and the curse of remembrance, du Maurier found a new way to extend her creativity in her late years. Her writing persona would actually transform into an ageing "other" that would nevertheless remain prolific until the very last years of her life. Through her writing, du Maurier forged her narrative identity in her old age, as her creative voice underwent a transformation, growing more inward-looking and even less self-assured but expanding nevertheless until she was well advanced in years.

REFERENCES

Beauvoir, Simone de. *The Coming of Age*. Trans. Patrick O'Brian. New York: Warner, 1973. Print.
Du Maurier, Daphne. "Don't Look Now." *Don't Look Now and Other Stories*. Harmondsworth: Penguin, 2006. 7-55. Print.
---. "Death and Widowhood." *The Rebecca Notebook and Other Writings*. London: Virago, 2004. 122-32. Print.
---. *Letters from Menabilly: Portrait of a Friendship*. Ed. Oriel Malet. London: Orion, 1994. Print.
---. *Growing Pains: The Shaping of a Writer*. London: Victor Gollancz, 1977. Print.
Forster, Margaret. *Daphne du Maurier*. London: Arrow, 1994. Print.
Horner, Avril, and Sue Zlosnik. "Glimpses of the Dark Side." *The Daphne du Maurier Companion*. Ed. Helen Taylor. London: Virago, 2007. 242-48. Print.
---. *Daphne du Maurier: Writing, Identity and the Gothic Imagination*. London: Macmillan, 1998. Print.
Kelly, Richard. *Daphne du Maurier*. Boston: Twayne, 1987. Print.
Ricoeur, Paul. *Memory, History, Forgetting*. Trans. Kathleen Blamey and David Pellauer. Chicago: U of Chicago P, 2006. Print.
---. *Oneself as Another*. Trans. Kathleen Blamey. Chicago: U of Chicago P, 1992. Print.
---. "Life in Quest of Narrative." *On Paul Ricoeur: Narrative and Interpretation*. Ed. David Wood. New York: Routledge, 1991. 20-33. Print.
---. "Narrative Identity." *On Paul Ricoeur: Narrative and Interpretation*. Ed. David Wood. New York: Routledge, 1991. 188-99. Print.
---. *Time and Narrative*. Vol. 2. Trans. Kathleen McLaughlin and David Pellauer. Chicago: U of Chicago P, 1985. Print.
Westland, Ella. *Reading Daphne*. Penryn: Truran, 2007. Print.
Woodward, Kathleen, and Murray Schwartz. "Introduction." *Memory and Desire: Ageing, Literature and Psychoanalysis*. Ed. Kathleen Woodward and Murray Schwartz. Bloomington: Indiana UP, 1986. 1-12. Print.

Ageing, Agency, and Autobiography
Challenging Ricoeur's Concept of Narrative Identity

RAHEL RIVERA GODOY-BENESCH

> Like any normal person, Tim Manning (speaking) used to think and speak of himself as "I," or "me" [...]. But that was Back Then.
> (BARTH, *THE DEVELOPMENT* 130)

In his collection *The Development* (2008), John Barth presents us with a character, Tim Manning, whose old age and incipient Alzheimer's disease pose a serious threat to his identity. Manning appears in two interrelated short stories, "Peeping Tom" and "Assisted Living," which both reveal his desperate attempts at re-defining his identity by writing his autobiography – despite his deteriorating memory. Indeed, in post-modern times, memory seems to be the *sine qua non* for any attempt to construct and affirm one's identity because it is the basis of narrative. Memory reaches back to the life experiences, to the points of orientation from which we can set out to construct a continuous and coherent life narrative that will result in a stable self-image. As Anthony Paul Kerby affirms in 1991:

[s]tudies ranging through sociology, psychology, philosophy, semiotics, literary theory, and historiography have taken up this interest in narrative, and it has become increasingly evident to numerous influential theorists and practitioners that narratives are a primary embodiment of our understanding of the world, of experience, and ultimately of ourselves. (3)

It is in this vein that Paul Ricoeur develops his concept of 'narrative identity' and integrates it into his theory of hermeneutics.[1] Narrative identity, for Ricoeur, is a response to the problem of integrating both change and permanence into a stable self-image. For this purpose, he divides identity into *idem* and *ipse*, the former roughly corresponding to sameness, which includes continuity and permanence over time, and the latter denoting selfhood, involving self-reflection and the telling of a life narrative to answer the question "Who am I?" ("Narrative Identity" 73-74).

Yet, as Patrick Crowley has shown, Ricoeur seems to avoid the immediate consequence of his approach, namely that narrative identity is most directly constituted by the act of writing autobiography. Crowley even suggests that "Ricoeur sidesteps autobiography in a bid to salvage narrative identity" (4) because "autobiography reveals the limits of Ricoeur's hermeneutic approach to texts" (6). What Crowley's discussion shows, at the very least, is that there seems to be a mismatch between Ricoeur's generalizing comments about life writing and the generic tradition of autobiography. Through a discussion of John Barth's Manning stories and Joan Didion's autobiographical writing, I would like to outline how the fixed narrative conventions of autobiography do indeed clash with Ricoeur's concept of narrative identity, especially in narratives of old age. Ricoeur's "presupposition that language is at man's disposal in the pursuit of meaning" (Crowley 8) – his deep belief in personal agency in constructing identity – prevents him from recognizing that narrative texts, whether they are fictional or autobiographical, are subject to formal restrictions. To a certain extent, writers and readers in pursuit of narrative identity must subordinate themselves to these limitations of narrative structure and genre and cannot dispose of the text as freely as critics and theorists in the aftermath of Postmodernism and Deconstruction would have it.

In narratives of old age, these generic restrictions are coupled with an even greater limitation, that of old age itself, which involves, firstly, the ever-lurking threat of death and, secondly, a serious reduction of one's

---

[1] Patrick Crowley, in "Paul Ricoeur: The Concept of Narrative Identity, the Trace of Autobiography," provides an overview of how Ricoeur's concept of narrative identity changes over time. For my current purpose, I will exclusively refer to Ricoeur's 1991 article "Narrative Identity," which is his last text on the subject.

agency through physical decline. Unlike many narratives that portray young or middle-aged protagonists, texts about old age are not characterised by the urge to narrativise the past but by their strong concerns with the present and future because the problematic part of life – that part in need of the mediation of narrative – is happening in the here-and-now, with its most traumatic event, namely death, lying in the future. Ricoeur's focus on narrative as a "presentifying of the past" through memory (Currie 5) cannot entirely account for identity in old age.

The second limitation that narratives of old age address is the fear of losing personal agency because of the gradual decline of one's physical and mental faculties. According to Heiner Bus, narratives about old age work against "the fear of ongoing decline and of eventual stasis" in trying to produce "the strong illusion of actively controlling fate" (186). Creating such a narrative can be considered a way of counteracting the loss of control and reduction of personal agency in old age. This presupposes, however, a strong dualist view of mind and body (if not a strictly Cartesian stance), which will not hold in old age, when the brain itself is affected by physical decline (Hughes, Louw and Sabat 7-8). There is a fundamental paradox in attempting to assert one's identity through narrative in old age because that approach is entirely dependent on a functioning mind. Stephen G. Post, who in 1995 coined the now oft-quoted term 'hypercognitivism' to denounce our society's tendency to determine a person's worth exclusively by considering his or her mental and rational capacities, calls for a new assessment of personal identity and suggests placing a higher value on emotional factors (232). The contemporary dominance of theories which postulate that identity must be actively and willingly constructed by the thinking subject has led to a situation in which the elderly, and most especially those affected by dementia, are increasingly isolated from the rest of society. This otherness of old age when it comes to the construction of identity is certainly a central topic in the two Manning stories by Barth: When Manning eventually presents his old age as different from "Back Then," when he "used to think and speak of himself as 'I,' or 'me'" like a "normal person" (*The Development* 130), the text asserts that the constitution of narrative identity through the agency of the mind is seriously threatened by old age.

With the character of Tim Manning, a former historian who is on the verge of losing his memory but nevertheless decides to write his autobiography, Barth has created difficult conditions indeed for a narrative to emerge. Yet it is precisely Barth's way of pushing things to their limits that exposes the issues that are at stake in narratives of old age. The loss of memory as a result of the ageing process, commonly referred to by the umbrella term 'dementia,' functions as a means of exploring the borderlines of storytelling. Narrative with its temporal (though not necessarily chronological) succession of events must build on memory not only for its telling but also for its reception. Dementia in Barth is not only used to probe deep into the secrets of narrative, it also serves as a metonymy for old age in general in that it emphasises the break with the former stages of life because the past becomes difficult to access. Such a "loss of temporal glue," to use Post's words (231), is usually associated with age-related illness rather than with normal, non-pathological ageing. As Hughes, Louw, and Sabat explain, when it comes to dementia, "it turns out there is no hard scientific boundary between disease and normality" (2). Following this latter view, I would like to suggest that Barth uses a narrator struck by dementia in order to *overemphasise* the condition of old age and so reveal the fundamental problems in narrativising old age (rather than comment on a particular disease). Manning's paradoxical project of writing his life story despite his deficient memory becomes paradigmatic of the difficulty to construct one's narrative identity in old age.

It is quite evident that Manning's autobiographical project in the first story, "Peeping Tom," which consists of an attempt to faithfully and truthfully record what happens in his neighbourhood "before [his] memory goes kaput altogether" (*The Development* 7), is meant to represent an overly simplistic understanding of autobiography. However, Manning himself at that stage seems to be convinced that he will succeed in drawing a faithful portrait of his reality through his narration, and he insists that he is no story-teller but rather "a history-teller" (7) and a "self-appointed chronicler" (22). In his obsession with truth he even reveals, in the nature of confessional writing, a shameful sexual secret to "put that discreditable aberration behind [him]" (21-22). That Barth equips Manning with the profession of a history teacher is certainly no coincidence. In his somewhat naïve approach to life-writing, rather than constructing his narrative identity, Manning carries out the work of a historian as Ricoeur describes it in *Time and Narrative III*. According to Ricoeur, historians "constitute signs as traces" in that they establish a temporal relationship between the past action that has left the sign and the here-and-now in which the sign still persists (124-26). Although Ricoeur's primary examples of such traces are historical documents in archives, Manning's way of dealing with his memory traces can be read as just such an attempt at building a temporal continuity between his past as a healthy middle-aged man – at the time when the signs became apparent – and his present in which these traces still persist in his memory. Whereas historical documents can be archived over a long time if they are kept in good climatic conditions, the condition of Manning's mental archive is deteriorating rapidly, and the memories are threatened. Manning's act of truthfully recounting his experiences is not only a historian's work of following traces back to the past action that generated them. By way of his autobiographical writing he generates new traces which will be safe from the erasure that his memories must eventually undergo.

Treating one's own life as if it were history comes with some uncomfortable consequences which give this approach to autobiography an air of mortality. Manning soon discovers the weaknesses of his history-based approach to writing and wishes that he could "follow [his account of his middle age] now with a proper dramatic climax and denouement" instead of the anti-climax of old age. He also notices that his history lacks closure and, addressing his reader, declares: "[W]hat You're winding up here, if You happen to exist, is a history, not a story, and its 'ending' is no duly gratifying Resolution nor even a capital-E Ending, really, just a sort of petering out, like most folks' lives" (22). He realises that history-writing, in addition to strict truthfulness, demands continuity, which will inevitably lead from his happy middle age to old age and his eventual death. This seems to echo Hemingway's famous statement that "all stories, if continued far enough, end in death, and he is no true-story teller who would keep that from you" (122). One of the fundamental problems of Manning's historical approach to autobiography then is that it triggers an understanding of time as a continuous, linear movement that will only create closure through the death of the protagonist. Despite the shortcomings of a 'history,' Manning's narrative serves its function of retrospectively stabilizing the writer's identity as a healthy middle-aged man. The fact that Manning's autobiographical narrative in "Peeping Tom" is not merely an act of securing that part of identity which Ricoeur defines as "the uninterrupted continuity in the development of being" (*Time and Narrative III* 74) but constitutes a desperate attempt to salvage his past in view of his frightening disease makes us react less condescendingly to his effort to truthfully reflect reality by use of language.

In fact, in the second story, "Assisted Living," it becomes perfectly clear why Manning placed so much emphasis on the truthfulness of his first account in "Peeping Tom." Only on the basis of this stable past identity can he set out to narrate his present, which is dominated by insecurity, weakness, and decline and for which he must adopt a more flexible writing strategy – a third-person narrative. This shift from "I" to "he" is a theoretically loaded movement. As Ricoeur almost too casually notes, "all grammatical persons are subject to ascription," which denotes the assignment of an agent to an action ("Narrative Identity" 75). Distinct pronouns indicate distinct actions that are performed by the self in its use of language. Whereas Ricoeur assigns "confession, the acceptance of responsibility (I did it)" to the first-person pronoun, the third person is, according to Ricoeur, used for narrative purposes (75). What we can conclude from these remarks is that the ascription in a confession in first-person form consists of the direct linking of (life) action and (speaking) agent, something proper of autobiography. The third-person form, in turn, creates a link between the speaking subject and the *action of narration* rather than the lived experience. In third-person narration, the subject constitutes itself not as a *living individual*, but as a *speaking voice*. Manning's turn from first-person to third-person narration thus signals that he has set out to find his speaking voice, which will allow him to construct his narrative identity in old age. He accordingly presents himself as "Tim Manning (speaking)" (130) and places strong emphasis on the present act of narration. But what will be the link between the here-and-now of this speaking voice and his lived reality, especially his past? Al-though the third-person narrative constitutes Ricoeur's *ipse* (the self-reflecting part of identity), how is Manning to secure the *idem* – that part of identity that stands for sameness, continuity and permanence over time – if the bridges to the past are burnt?

Barth is a clever craftsman when it comes to narrative structure, and he provides Manning with some of his skill as becomes evident right at the beginning of Manning's second story. To establish the permanence over time that is needed for the *idem*, Manning integrates the durable traces of his first story, "Peeping Tom," (the passages in italics) into his second story, "Assisted Living":

Like any normal person, Tim Manning (speaking) used to think and speak of himself as "I," or "me." *Don't ask me*, the old ex-history teacher would start off one of his "His-Stories" by typing on his computer, *who I think is reading or hearing this* – and then on he'd ramble about his and Margie's Oyster Cove community in Heron Bay Estates, and the interesting season when they and their neighbourhood were bedeviled (or at least had reason to believe they were) by a Peeping Tom. Stuff like that. *I grabbed the big flashlight from atop the fridge*, he would write, *told Margie to call Security, and stepped out back to check*. Or *"I do sort of miss those days," Margie said to me one evening a few years later ...*
That sort of thing.
But that was Back Then [.] (130)

The new form of Tim Manning's quest for narrative identity is a merger of the *action of living* of his first narrative and the *action of writing* of his second one, a merger of history and narrative, autobiography and fiction, and he accordingly calls it a "His-Story" (131). The real master stroke, however, is that the third-person narrator who tells the second story is "T.M." – the I-narrator of Manning's first story, who is stable and reliable and bases his autobiographical narrative on mere facts. In some sense then Manning employs his former, stable self to deal with the illness of his present, weak self.

This outsourcing of the narrator – Manning calls it *assisted living* in analogy with the assisted living residence to which he and his wife have moved – is a last resort to hold on to the idea of narrative identity in old age, but the permanence over time that Manning's approach attempts to secure is double-edged. Although the quotations from his former story, the traces, are present in the current story, and although the narrator still consists of Tim Manning, or "T.M.," the story's self is a different one linguistically as he shifts from first-person to third-person narration. Manning's effort to create continuity, paradoxically, both confirms and refutes permanence over time. His commentary that "Back Then" he could use the first-person pronoun to refer to himself "[l]ike any normal person" (130) powerfully illustrates this paradox: it acknowledges the past at the same moment as it invokes a break with it. That Manning considers his middle age to have been the normal stage of his life, as opposed to old age, implies that old age is abnormal, odd, and other. This otherness of the last stage of life does not just refer to identity; it should be read primarily as a comment on the writing of autobiography.

Barth's two Manning stories make a number of important statements about old age, identity, and autobiography, and the protagonist's strategy of outsourcing narrative agency by employing his stable, middle-aged self is, at first sight, a clever solution to the problems at hand. To tell one's life narrative through a narrator who is an image of one's former self, however, challenges and inverts the very premise of autobiography. As Smith and Watson propose in their comprehensive study of autobiography, the narrator of the autobiographical text consists of a narrating "I" (the first-person narrator) and a narrated "I," which coincides with the protagonist (72-75).[2] What follows from Smith and Watson's proposal is that autobiographical narratives presuppose a temporal distance between the narrating "I" and the narrated "I," as the former talks about the latter in the past tense. In addition to this temporal distance, the narrating "I" also distances itself from the narrated "I" by its having more knowledge and maturity. That the narrating "I" already knows how the story of the narrated "I" will end results in the ironic structure inherent in every autobiographical narrative. In "Assisted Living," Manning's use of his former, middle-aged self to control his present, debilitated narrated "I" illustrates this need for a narrator who is superior to the character.

Yet, due to its paradoxical temporal set-up, his narrative construct is doomed to fail. In the most common form of autobiography, the ironic distance between narrating "I" and narrated "I" diminishes towards the end of the narrative, and the two entities might even merge and the hierarchy collapse as the temporal distance becomes shorter and shorter as the story advances. Mark Currie has noted a similar temporal effect in confessional novels and he observes that "[s]elf-distance must end in self-presence as the events of a life catch up with the moment of telling it" (61). In "Assisted Living," however, as time passes and the story progresses, the temporal distance between the ageing narrated "I" (i.e. old Manning) and its static, middle-aged narrator increases. The narrated "I" does not approach the

---

2   This is a somewhat reductive rendering of Smith and Watson's model but it is sufficient for my purpose.

narrating "I" in terms of cognitive development either. On the contrary, due to Manning's age-related decline, the cognitive gap widens. In short – and to come back to Ricoeur's terms – the more Manning's narrative of old age develops, the farther away he moves from a reconciliation of *ipse* and *idem*. It is a serious, if not a shocking, revelation about old-age autobiography that arises in the Manning stories, but Barth offers a partial solution: Manning's turn from history to "His-Story" also involves a turn towards fictionalizing old age. If autobiography cannot result in a stable identity in old age, then old age must be invented.

According to Philippe Lejeune's groundbreaking, yet not uncontroversial, work on autobiography, the crucial difference between fictional narratives and autobiography, and therefore the latter's main distinguishing feature, is that the names of narrator, protagonist, and author coincide, and the author therefore enters a so-called 'autobiographical pact' with the reader, which will either bind him/her to absolute truthfulness or else characterise his/her narrative as a lie (16-18). In other words, in autobiographical narratives, the life of the real-life author, whom Smith and Watson call a historical "I" (72), is of prime importance, whereas in fiction it has been marginal at best since the New Critics' invocation of intentional fallacy and Roland Barthes's declaration of the death of the author. Yet, as Frédéric Regard rightly states, in biographical writing, "the notion of the author's concrete life as a person, a living individual, cannot be totally eradicated from the literary text" (396) and the "maxim of the text as a 'neutral space' is challenged" (399).

It is precisely this return to, or return of, the author that Manning is trying to avoid when he switches to a fictional story with narrator "T.M." in charge because he recognises that he, as the author, no longer has the mental capacity to construct a coherent narrative. This would threaten the primary goal of his narrative, which is to write *against* mental decline, *against* approaching decay and death. His narrative is supposed to mediate his old age by providing an illusion of the stability and coherence that the narrator "T.M." stands for. Writing fiction, which consists of building an artificial, alternative world with the neat structure of narrative, appears to be the right activity for such an enterprise. However, what looks like a sound plan ends in disaster, and Manning's second narrative is not a coherent story at all: more than once, the narrator digresses, forgets what "'Tim Manning' was about to say before this particular His-Story wandered," (131) and breaks off abruptly. His text turns into a patchwork of old memories, present worries, and pieces of the recent past, all of which is characterised by an increasing tone of hopelessness and despair. The story "Assisted Living" becomes the mirror image of Tim Manning as an old man – the true image of its author. Ultimately, the Manning stories suggest that no structural entity in the literary text can entirely dissociate itself from the real author, not even in fiction. The boundary between fiction and autobiography must therefore be questioned, and the author becomes a core point to consider in both due to his position as the narrative's agent.

This affirmation of the author's agency is central to narratives that deal with old age no matter whether they are autobiographical or fictional. It is certainly no coincidence that Roland Barthes relativised his declaration of the death of the author and turned to the theory of autobiography precisely as he was growing old. In fact, the lecture in which he theorised about the "return of the author" and the "return to biography" ("Life as Work" 207-09) took place only a few weeks before his death. It seems that, in the final stages of life, when control over the body and the mind is decreasing, it becomes particularly important to affirm personal agency. This is readily apparent in many aged authors' writing and it partially manifests itself in their desperate affirmation of authorial control over their texts. The fact that many authors in old age turn to either autobiographical writing or to a fictional portrait of the aged artist,[3] moreover, makes this return to the author quite palpable at the level of content. The long descriptions of these protagonists' physical weaknesses and illnesses especially mark the presence and significance of authors as real persons. They foreground their corporality and, in focusing on the ephemeral nature of human existence, their historicity. As the bodies of the aged characters – and quite often of the authors themselves – take centre stage, these texts express a struggle against their authors' reduction to a mere speaking voice.

Nevertheless, it is only language that can be displayed in a text. As Patricia Waugh states in reference to "Night Sea Journey," one of Barth's early short stories, "[the character's] embodiment longed for is of

---

3   Numerous writers could be listed like Mark Twain, Joseph Heller, Philip Roth, J. M. Coetzee, Karen Blixen, Carson McCullers, Joan Didion, besides Cervantes and Shakespeare – indeed, who not?

something outside language, beyond an author, but it is of course the author's 'voice' which is the utterance; language which is the totality of existence; text which is reality." Waugh's statement accurately describes the paradox of a *fictional* character, who "both exists and does not exist" (91) in the writer's and the reader's reality, but, in autobiographical narratives, the fact is that the protagonist does in some way exist as a real person, which shows us quite plainly that there is an anterior reality outside language. For autobiography, we need to adjust Waugh's assertion: What is longed for is not the character's embodiment outside language – which is a given – but the convergence of language and physical, anterior reality. What is at stake is the representative function of language rather than its creative force.

This point at which the reality of the author and the language of his or her text meet, however, can never be reached, as the Manning stories suggest, because the narration of the past can never catch up with the author's present. As soon as Manning realises that the story he is writing will not improve his situation, will not "assist" his "living" in any way, he gives up. Increasingly confused, he only sees one possibility for ending his life in a dignified way before his mental disease takes over completely: He decides, in a last act of the will, to force closure upon his narrative identity through his own death:

Assisted Living? Been there, done that.
So?
Well. Somewhere on this QWERTYUIOP keyboard – maybe up among all those *F1-F12, pg up/pg dn, num lock/clear* buttons? – there ought to be one for Assisted Dying ...
Like, hey, one of these, maybe: *<home? end>?*
help
Worth a try:
enter. (140)

The story virtually takes over the old man's identity, and after these last words, Manning does not make any more appearances in the interrelated short stories of *The Development*. Ricoeur's statement that "the story of a life continues to be refigured by all the truthful or fictive stories a subject tells about himself or herself" (*Time and Narrative III* 246) is pushed to its limit. Moreover, Barth exposes the enterprise of representing identity through narrative as deeply troubled. The ending of "Assisted Living" suggests that narration cannot account for identity in the here-and-now but only retrospectively mediate memories: At the moment in which the story reaches the present, and the narrated "I" from the past is about converge with its narrating "I," that is, in Ricoeur's words, when *idem* and *ipse* should arrive at a harmonic overlap, Manning's narrative construct breaks down. Manning's death as a character, as a narrator, and, most importantly, as the author of his life story provides the text with the closure we long for, but we should not forget that this is only possible because he is a fictional character and not a real person.

Still, what this analysis shows is that to constitute one's identity through narrative by foregrounding the author's life, especially through autobiography or near-autobiography, clashes with a genre-specific temporality, which in focusing solely on the past may run counter to the narrative's aim of coming to terms with a problematic present and future. The writing of a life story in autobiography, with its hierarchical relationship between the narrating "I" and the narrated "I," relies heavily on the generic tradition of the novel in the form of a *Bildungsroman*, whose basic narrative development is that of a protagonist overcoming his or her socially difficult youth and arriving at his or her integration into society. Coming-of-age stories provide narrative closure by concluding with the protagonist having achieved a stabilised identity. What is important to note is that these stories present the temporality of the protagonist's ageing as a form of progress in its most positive sense; the advancing of time signifies a journey towards a higher level of understanding, which coincides with narrative closure as the story ends. It follows that past and present are endowed with negative and positive connotations, respectively, and the linearity of the development from a problematic past to a stable present projects our expectations beyond the ending point of the story into the promise of a bright future, which is often epitomised by the protagonist's marriage and carries an overtone of the 'ever after' happy ending of fairy tales. From this point of view, the narrative tradition of the novel of development is quite unsuitable for coming to terms with old age because the advancing of time in old age has entirely different connotations and the values of past and future are reversed. Although it could be argued that structures can be revised and adapted, even such highly experimental texts as Barth's Manning stories show that long-standing historical traditions of writing cannot easily be overcome.

Two of the most highly praised – and prized – literary autobiographies of recent years, Joan Didion's *The Year of Magical Thinking* (2005) and *Blue Nights* (2011), shall serve to illustrate that not only fictional characters, but also real-life writers in old age experience problems with this traditional temporality of the novel. Shortly after Didion, then in her sixties, had begun her autobiographical project with *Where I Was From* (2003), in which she retells her family history and the story of her own youth in the fashion of a *Bildungsroman*, her husband unexpectedly died from a stroke. To assimilate this identity-threatening event, Didion wrote *The Year of Magical Thinking*, which was highly successful both as a novel and as a play. *Blue Nights* (2011), in striking contrast to her earlier personality, portrays Didion as a frail and dispirited old writer who must realise that the narration of old age is subject to different temporal conventions than the ones of which she had made successful use in *The Year of Magical Thinking*.

The Year of Magical Thinking assumes the shape of a trauma narrative with that genre's typical structure as James Phelan convincingly exposes: "As the narrative progresses, the distance between the narrating-I and the [narrated-I] diminishes until, finally, they converge" in their acceptance of the traumatic event, Didion's husband's sudden death (129). In *Blue Nights*, Didion sets out to apply the same procedure to the assimilation of her daughter's tragic death in 2005. Yet, as the narrative progresses, Didion must recognise that she is not really writing about her daughter's illness and death but about her own increasing frailty. Old age literally intrudes upon her plans for the narrative in the form of the phrase "time passes," which interrupts her memories several times (13-17). Whereas Didion first believes that this phrase means that "memory adjusts, memory conforms to what we think we remember" (13), she finally comes to realise that the almost compulsively written phrase "time passes" actually points to her growing old, to the "irreversible changes in mind and body" and to "[t]he way in which your awareness of this passing time – this permanent slowing, this vanishing resilience – multiplies, metastasises, becomes your very life" (17). The passing of time mutates from a healing process through the thinking mind's willing adjustment of memory to a sickening, involuntary confrontation with one's ageing process and eventual death – a painful exercise that does not result in any stable identity in the sense of a consolidation of *idem* and *ipse*.

One can, of course, argue that the confrontation of the age-related frailty and the prospect of dying – in Didion's words, the "fear of what is still to be lost" (*Blue Nights* 188) – is precisely what the narrative should undertake, and that although it cannot resolve the trauma of old age it does fulfil its purpose by merely addressing it. Ricoeur, in "Narrative Identity," acknowledges that narratives, especially what he calls the modern novels, do not necessarily lead to a stable identity but instead explore "all the intermediary combinations between the complete overlap of identity-as-sameness and identity-as-ipseity" or even stage "the complete dissociation between the two modalities of identity" (78).

In old-age narratives, the difficulty of reaching an overlap of *idem* and *ipse* – in contrast to conventional trauma narratives, which aim at integrating the traumatic event into the timeline of one's life – lies in the fact that the trauma of old age cannot be reduced to an event in the past. The writer cannot make use of the adaptive function of memory to retrospectively transform the traumatic moment. Furthermore, the progressive nature of age-related decline calls for a continuous adaptation of the story's content and narrative strategy resulting in closure being continuously postponed. In Didion's case, her realizing that her own frailty and death are the actual subjects of her writing leads to a completely different writing strategy, and she abandons her initial narrative in the past tense, at first for a fragmented narration of present events and eventually in favour of a poetry-like style with verse lines. These lines, which instead of recounting life events express Didion's reflections about her fear of death, can be viewed as an attempt to avoid linear temporality by abandoning her life narrative because poetry traditionally harbours the illusion of suspended time and the promise of eternity. Narrative in the sense of a temporal succession of events does not assist Didion in constituting her identity in old age (Ricoeur's "emplotment"). Rather, it is the affirmation of herself as a thinking subject, a lyrical "I," who is still in control of her writing. What is important for maintaining a stable identity is the mere act of writing as a "signifying practice" (Kerby 1) rather than the narrative content with its temporal plot that would ideally unite *idem* and *ipse*. Identity arises from a present action, and the question 'Who am I?' can be safely answered by 'This is what I do – now.' Whether this conclusion holds just for the limited space of *Blue Nights* or for Didion herself as well is questionable. In 2011, aged 76 and talking about the difficulties she experienced while writing *Blue Nights*, Didion said: "I used to say I was a writer, but it's less up front now. Maybe because it didn't help me." The fact that "she's not sure whether she will write again" seems to confirm her crisis of identity (Tuhy 42).

What Barth's fictional short stories and Didion's autobiographical writing suggest is that old age is, apparently, incompatible with the narrative mode for constituting one's identity. Ricoeur, in stating that "so many modern autobiographies [...] distance themselves from the narrative form and rejoin a literary genre that is much less configured, namely the essay" ("Narrative Identity" 78), partly acknowledges that identity in crisis leads to that disintegration of narrative. However, he holds that only identity-as-sameness reveals itself to be in crisis and that the literary text, no matter how fragmented or essayistic it appears, is still representative of ipseity by merely expressing the question "Who am I?" (78). The immediate consequence of his affirmation is that the whole quest for narrative identity can only succeed if identity is *not* in crisis. And even there one could certainly argue that despite Ricoeur's phenomenological perspective, narrative identity is only a verbal illusion, produced by a mind with excellent analytic qualities and a considerable amount of ironic self-distance, one endowed with enough flexibility to engage in a playful exercise with language. This excludes the elderly, who are not only affected by weakened sensory perceptions but very often also (eventually) by a faltering mind. Ricoeur therefore inscribes himself in the tradition of hypercognitivism that is so sharply criticised by Post. His construction of "an ethical notion of narrative identity that privileges agency" (Crowley 1) seems to rely on the same, outdated assumptions that Smith and Watson observe in early attempts at theorizing autobiography in the 1960s, namely that the writer was "an autonomous and enlightened 'individual' who exercised free will" (199). Even for writers like Didion, who are still fully in command of their minds and writing, this playfulness and readiness to engage in imagination and illusions in "the thought experiments set before us by literature" (Ricoeur, "Narrative Identity" 80), may no longer be available in view of more immediate problems at hand, such as illness, pain, and loss. I would therefore go so far as to suggest that setting out to constitute one's narrative identity in old age, in contrast to Ricoeur's insistence on the "purgative virtue, in the sense of Aristotelian Catharsis" (80), can lead to a more profound crisis because it unnecessarily brings those aspects of ageing to the fore that are uncontrollable, namely the advancing of time and the body's decline.

The question that still needs to be addressed is in what ways insights into the limitations of narrative identity may be relevant not only to old-age narratives, particularly autobiography, but also to other kinds of life writing. Initially, Ricoeur's strong focus on memory and the narration of the past, together with his and many other scholars' assumption that Jean Paul Sartre's proposition that "existence precedes essence" (348) holds true, looks like the perfect premise for a successful construction of narrative identity in old age because the thinking subject has a long past at his or her disposal. Such a panoramic view of one's life, through which single, identity-threatening events may be relativised and a more stable, whole image might emerge, however, presupposes a critical distance from this past. The resulting break between past and present, between the lived life and the thinking subject, whether in a strictly temporal sense or from a philosophical point of view that emphasises the division between body and mind, becomes apparent in the study of autobiography when trying to pinpoint the moment at which the narrating "I" and the narrated "I" overlap because this moment can only ever take place in the illusory space of the text. The narrative, then, does not contribute to the subject's constitution of identity, but it functions as a temporary compensation for the impossibility of ever reaching a stable identity, a fact we seem to be ready to accept for most of our lives. So far, there is no apparent reason why these observations should not apply to life narratives at any stage.

What is arguably different about old age is that this impossible, illusory convergence of the living and the speaking subject becomes an ever more pressing matter as the decline of the body sets in, and reality is in acute need of mediation by language. The turn to autobiography in many aged authors' writing and the extensive catalogues of illnesses and declining faculties that characterise both fictional and non-fictional aged characters suggest that the present realities of old age constitute a higher threat to the subjects' identities than their possibly fragmented pasts. The role of narrative to provide access to one's self – in however a reductionist approach – and facilitate the understanding of the human experience should be seriously questioned, but the yearning for precisely this representative and explanatory function of language and literature remains intact. From the point of view of ageing studies, a hermeneutic approach to texts that holds that the mere act of reading *is* life and can transform life (Ricoeur, "Life in Quest of Narrative" 27) seems almost cynical. How will a text be able to counter pain and assist elderly people in handling the daily chores that have become so difficult? How will mental exercise improve physical reality? In this sense, narratives of old age, in Bus's words, can only "[record] failures and decline with some small and provisional victories which is all there is" (186-87).

The ongoing boom of old-age narratives and the increasing critical attention they are receiving contest this sobering outlook to some extent. This development might, however, also reinforce the separation between the ones who are still the agents of their lives – the thinkers with a functioning mind – and those whose illness and decline have taken over. The growing popularity of dividing old age into two stages, third and fourth, by clearly separating the active and creative part of the aged population from those who have begun the descent towards death can be considered quite symptomatic. Old-age research that aims at improving independence and life satisfaction is a double-edged sword because it systematically denies the elderly their right to be and feel ill, to lose the agency of the mind, and hence to be cared for by younger generations. The fourth stage of life, where not only the body may be ill, but also the mind too weak to cope with reality by thinking up solutions, is not addressed. It is postponed and pushed to the margin. From this perspective it is also problematic that in 2011, Huber et al. (an impressive group of European and American researchers) put forward a proposal in the *British Medical Journal* to change the WHO definition of health and shift its focus from "complete wellbeing" to "the ability to adapt and self manage in the face of social, physical, and emotional challenges" (1). The terms "adapt" and "self manage" not only contain a dangerous potential for social-Darwinist thought but also suggest that health can be achieved by an autonomous effort of the mind, by the sheer exercise of free will. The other side of the coin is that illness and decline are implicitly defined as a lack of an individual's effort to "adapt and self manage," which in the worst case presents illness as one's own fault. With this definition, the authors inscribe themselves in a tradition that considers individuals to be the forgers of their own destiny, and it rules out those who have limited coping capacities, such as the elderly.

Literature, though it is produced by creative and functioning minds, has the potential to challenge this privileging of mental agency, which Post would classify as "hypercognitive snobbery" (223). Barth's Manning stories and Didion's autobiography, along with Roth's famous statement that "old age is a massacre" (156) and many other aged authors' refusal to euphemise physical and mental distress in old age, are therefore valuable, non-scientific contributions to ageing studies.

REFERENCES

Barth, John. *The Development*. Boston: Houghton Mifflin, 2008. Print.
---. "Night Sea Journey." *Lost in the Funhouse*. New York: Anchor, 1988. 3-13. Print.
Barthes, Roland. "Life as Work." *The Preparation of the Novel*. Trans. Kate Briggs. European Perspectives: A Series in Social Thought and Cultural Criticism. New York: Columbia UP, 2011. 207-11. Print.
---. "The Death of the Author." *Image, Music, Text*. Ed. and trans. Stephen Heath. London: Fontana, 1977. 142-48. Print.
Bus, Heiner. "Ageing in Recent Jewish-American Literature." *Old Age and Ageing in British and American Culture and Literature*. Ed. Christa Jansohn. Studien zur englischen Literatur 16. Münster: LIT, 2004. 173-87. Print.
Crowley, Patrick. "Paul Ricoeur: The Concept of Narrative Identity, the Trace of Autobiography." *Paragraph: A Journal of Modern Critical Theory* 26.3 (2003): 1-12. Print.
Currie, Mark. *About Time: Narrative, Fiction and the Philosophy of Time*. The Frontiers of Theory. Edinburgh: Edinburgh UP, 2007. Print.
Didion, Joan. *Blue Nights*. London: Harper, 2011. Print.
---. *The Year of Magical Thinking*. London: Harper, 2011. Print.
---. *Where I Was From: A Memoir*. London: Harper, 2004. Print.
Hemingway, Ernest. *Death in the Afternoon*. New York: Touchstone, 1996. Print.
Huber, Machteld, et al. "How Should We Define Health?" *British Medical Journal* 343.4163 (2011): 1-3. Print.

Hughes, Julian C., Stephen C. Louw, and Steven R. Sabat. "Seeing Whole." *Dementia: Mind, Meaning, and the Person*. Ed. Julian C. Hughes, Stephen C. Louw, and Steven R. Sabat. Oxford: Oxford UP, 2006. 1-20. Print.

Kerby, Anthony Paul. *Narrative and the Self*. Bloomington: Indiana UP, 1991. Print.

Lejeune, Philippe. *On Autobiography*. Ed. Paul John Eakin. Trans. Katherine Leary. Theory and History of Literature 52. Minneapolis: U of Minnesota P, 1989. Print.

Phelan, James. "The Implied Author, Deficient Narration, and Nonfiction Narrative: Or, What's Off-Kilter in *The Year of Magical Thinking* and *The Diving Bell and the Butterfly?*" *Style* 45.1 (2011): 119-37. Print.

Post, Stephen G. "*Respectare*: Moral Respect for the Lives of the Deeply Forgetful." *Dementia: Mind, Meaning, and the Person*. Ed. Julian C. Hughes, Stephen C. Louw, and Steven R. Sabat. Oxford: Oxford UP, 2006. 223-34. Print.

Regard, Frédéric. "The Ethics of Biographical Reading: A Pragmatic Approach." *Cambridge Quarterly* 29.4 (2000): 394-408. Print.

Ricoeur, Paul. "Life in Quest of Narrative." *On Paul Ricoeur: Narrative and Interpretation*. Ed. David Wood. London: Routledge, 1991. 20-33. Print.

---. "Narrative Identity." *Philosophy Today* 35.1 (1991): 73-81. Print.

---. *Time and Narrative*. Vol. 3. 1985. Trans. Kathleen Blamey and David Pellauer. Chicago: U of Chicago P, 1988. Print.

Roth, Philip. *Everyman*. Boston: Houghton, 2006. Print.

Sartre, Jean Paul. "Existentialism Is a Humanism." Trans. Philip Mairet. *Existentialism from Dostoevsky to Sartre*. Ed. Walter Kaufmann. New York: Meridian, 1956. 345-69. Print.

Smith, Sidonie, and Julia Watson. *Reading Autobiography: A Guide for Interpreting Life Narratives*. 2nd ed. Minneapolis, U of Minnesota P, 2010. Print.

Tuhy, Carrie. "JOAN DIDION Stepping into the River Styx, Again." *Publishers Weekly* 258.40 (2011): 41-42. Print.

Waugh, Patricia. *Metafiction: The Theory and Practice of Self-Conscious Fiction*. New Accents. London: Routledge. 2003. Print.

An Appetite for Life
Narrative, Time, and Identity in *Still Mine*

PAMELA GRAVAGNE

INTRODUCTION

"It doesn't seem like a day for a funeral, does it?" asks Irene.
"No, but I don't imagine many days do," Craig answers.
"Do you think much about dying?"
"Probably not as much as I should."
"When I was young, I looked at old people and thought, if you live long enough, you'll probably have time to figure out dying. But I'm no closer now to the great mystery than when I was ten," Irene admits.
"See that as a problem, do you?"
Looking wistfully out the window, Irene answers, "We'll find out – soon enough."
"Speak for yourself. I plan on beating the odds."

Irene's inability to come to terms with the concept of death and Craig's almost flippant unwillingness to spend too much time thinking about it in this brief scene from the beginning of the movie *Still Mine* (2013) embody well the personal experience of philosopher Paul Ricoeur (1913-2005) as he dealt with the approach of his own demise. While celebrating his ninetieth birthday, he confided to his close friend, Catherine Goldenstein, that, despite the toll that age and disease had taken on his body, "he was making 'great progress' in his reflections of our common 'having-to-die'" (Goldenstein 93). However, he added, until that day arrived, he intended to honour life by "living up to death" (94) with what he called "the grace of insouciance" (Abel xiii). His ambivalent attitude, combining both acceptance and refusal, manifested itself by times of nameless anxiety, "what he himself called a 'lucid depression'" when he felt he could no longer do his work of writing (Goldenstein 94), alternating with periods marked by a forceful reassertion of his will "to be there, alive" when he composed his last short, often fragmentary, texts (95).

While becoming "'capable of dying' was Ricoeur's present concern" (95), he approached the gap between "wanting to live and having to die" (*Memory, History, Forgetting* 358) in the same manner he had dealt in his previous work with the aporias, or irresolvable internal contradictions, of time and memory common to human existence. By examining and critiquing the ideas of other philosophers, he found ways to argue that apparently mutually exclusive conclusions actually depended on assumptions made by each other (*Time and Narrative III* 57). Therefore, rather than try to resolve the tensions between philosophical approaches to understanding the mysteries of life, Ricoeur made them productive. For example, Ricoeur brought Heidegger, for whom human authenticity was marked by a being-toward-death that placed all future experience in "the shadow of death" (*Memory, History, Forgetting* 250), into conversation with both Sartre, who characterised "death as the interruption of our potentiality-for-Being rather than as its most authentic possibility" (*Time and Narrative III* 67) and with Spinoza, who argued that one must "remain alive until and not for death" (*Memory, History, Forgetting* 357). From these seemingly antithetical positions, Ricoeur constructed an alternate understanding of dying in which, even though the knowledge of death might be internalised and accepted, this knowledge would always remain "frightening, anguishing, precisely because of its radical heterogeneity in relation to our desire" and to our flesh (358). Strengthened by the testimony of physicians specializing in palliative care who noted that even the dying and the soon to be dead continue to see themselves as "still living" (*Time and Narrative III* 14) and by his inability to imagine his own death, Ricoeur's understanding led him to conclude that one can never "stop pulling oneself together, seeking 'who' one is, mobilizing one's forces, one's memories, one's desire, in an appetite for life" (Abel xi).

Collected in the small volume *Living Up to Death*, these texts and fragments on the subject of death, dying, and, ultimately, life are clearly a continuation of Ricoeur's long-term project of phenomenological hermeneutics or of making human existence both intelligible and meaningful. The intelligibility and meaning that we all desire, Ricoeur argued, can only be attained by resolving the two-dimensional character of human experience through the use of narrative. The resources of narrative, he wrote, can mediate the discordance we feel between our infinite freedom of will and the finite fact of our existence, our non-chronological private experience of inner time and the chronological linear public time in which our lives unfold, and our continuing involvement with an absent past that remains present to us through memory, history, and both material and psychic traces. Moreover, the mediation accomplished through narrative gives us the ability to synthesise the raw and often unconnected events of biological life with the asynchronicity of our inner time to develop a story and to construct an identity that we call our "self." And since narrative is always open to interpretation and reinterpretation, Ricoeur continued, both our story and our "self" are also open to re-examination and revision throughout our lives and the lives of those for whom we live on in memory.

Although Ricoeur most often illustrated his philosophical arguments on narrative and time through literary example and critique, he also believed in the power of film to bring philosophy into contact with life by giving "the illusion of presence" to human events through time (Ricoeur, "Memory, History, Forgiveness" 16). In this paper, I examine how Paul Ricoeur's concepts of narrative, time, and narrative identity can be used to analyse the way that ageing and old age are portrayed in the movie *Still Mine*. Based on a true story about the efforts of Irene and Craig, an octogenarian couple, to maintain their independence as she slips ever deeper into dementia, the story told in *Still Mine* lucidly illustrates three of the main ideas Ricoeur presents in *Time and Narrative III* and *Memory, History, Forgetting*. The first concerns the manner in which narrative combines history (the attempt to recreate events that actually happened) with fiction (the fabrication of an imaginative world surrounding these events) in order to create narrated or human time. The second explores the ability of human time to construct a "lived" temporality that mediates between the objectivity of cosmological time and the subjectivity of phenomenological time and with the potential of human time to bridge the temporal distance between past and present. The last investigates the power of this "lived" temporality to endow a person with both a coherent life story and a narrative identity that, though perceived as a stable inward sense of self, is open to revision throughout life. The events depicted in *Still Mine,* I argue, deal directly with the ability, and the desire, of older people to continue to narratively reconfigure their lives despite the vicissitudes of growing older. Through the lens of Ricoeur's ideas, I conclude that this film exemplifies, and offers an opportunity to experience as Ricoeur himself did, the concept of the dynamic circularity between narrative and the appetite for life.

HISTORY AND FICTION IN HUMAN TIME

The film opens with a shot of Craig attempting to neatly tie his necktie. Next the camera slowly rises to a close up of his face, his age clearly marked on its craggy features, as he combs his thinning hair with his hand. The scene then abruptly shifts to a courthouse where we hear that Craig, who is in violation of a court order to stop construction of the new house he is building, may face jail time due to twenty-six failures to comply with building regulations. His expression remarkably composed, Craig pauses, then asks the judge, "Are you a baseball fan, your honor?" Rather than hear the judge's answer, the words "two years earlier" appear across a black screen and we are transported to a rocky beach where Craig is standing, looking pensively out at the water. As we watch Craig standing silently on that beach, we hear his voice telling the story of the baseball game his father took him to see when he was eleven. It was at that game, Craig tells us, that he managed to get both Babe Ruth and Lou Gehrig to sign his now famous, and valuable, baseball. Leaving this scene, we suddenly find ourselves at a family picnic where Craig, stunned by his nine-year-old grandson's lack of knowledge about Babe Ruth, is caught short when his grandson equates Craig's lack of knowledge about contemporary figures important to nine-year olds to his own ignorance about Babe Ruth. At this point, although we, as an audience, are not yet fully aware of the significance of baseball in the narrative, through the imaginative use of what Ricoeur calls narrative emplotment, or the configuration of temporally discordant objects, events, and persons into an order that endows them with both meaning and the appearance of necessity, we already know that baseball will have an important role to play as the story unfolds.

From the first scenes, *Still Mine* interweaves history and fiction by depicting or telling about actual events of Craig and Irene's lives – in a courtroom, at a game, and at a picnic – then rearranging them into a coherent narrative or plot that appears to conform to the logic of cause and event. Ricoeur clarifies the importance of this imaginative reconfiguration of human actions and events in his discussion on the reciprocal overlapping of history and fiction. Describing history as a desire to accurately re-present or stand for the past (*Memory, History, Forgetting* 274) by examining evidence of "situations, events, connections, and characters who once really existed" (275) found in testimony, documents, or archives, Ricoeur emphasises the interpretive nature of historical re-creation. Guided by a particular project, question, or hypothesis, a historian, novelist, or filmmaker, says Ricoeur, chooses which traces, or actual material reminders or remnants of the past, such as a baseball, she or he will allow to "speak" and which will remain mute. The facts ascertained from these archival "voices" are not positivistic facts that correspond directly to what actually occurred but are themselves interpretations of the traces ("Paul Ricoeur" *Stanford Encyclopedia*). A trace, Ricoeur continues, only becomes "an actual operator of historical time" when "we provide ourselves with a figure of the world surrounding the relic [through] the activity of the imagination" (*Time and Narrative III* 184). It is by means of fiction with its ability to rearrange events using the devices of emplotment, he argues, that we construct a narrative of what *was,* such as a movie based on a true story that can believably stand for the past.

A similar process takes place in the creation of fiction, Ricoeur maintains. As history calls for fictionalization "in the service of standing for the past," fiction historicises narratives, recounting them *as if* they were past (189). In order for the "as if past" to be believable, the fictional narrative must be probable or necessary and "must have a relation of verisimilitude to what has been" recounted before (191). According to Ricoeur, since fiction includes both the actualities of the historical or "real" past (the game and the signed baseball) and the potentialities of the fictive or "unreal" past (the use of the baseball to connect apparently unconnected events into a larger whole), then, like history, fiction is bound to the past by the necessity of verisimilitude even though it can be free from the constraints of the archive or trace. It is this reciprocal overlapping or blending of history and fiction, argues Ricoeur, that gives rise to what he calls narrated or human time. Because the production of human time cannot be assigned exclusively to either historical or fictional narrative, it has the ability to span the gap between the virtual worlds of imagination and the actual world of acting and suffering. Human time can close this distance, argues Ricoeur, by the way it enables narrative to pass through the three stages of what he calls mimesis. In stage one, a narrative is understood and structured in a culturally significant symbolic form; in stage two, it is configured into a meaningful whole that adheres to the continuity demanded by life; and in the last stage, it may be integrated into one's identity and self understanding, a process that enables the world of a text to transcend itself in the direction of a lived world (*Time and Narrative III* 158). By dissolving the opposition between the "inside of fiction" and the "outside of life" (Valdes 15) through mimesis, human time, "to the extent that it is articulated through a narrative mode" (19), is open to "an unending process of revision" (*Memory, History, Forgetting* 234) and becomes a living, continuous story.

Because it is open to imaginative revision, the production of human time resulting from narrative emplotment must mediate between what Ricoeur calls two elementary senses of time: cosmological time, which unfolds as undifferentiated and equal moments into a seemingly endless future, and phenomenological time, in which some moments of a brief life are more meaningful than others. This new temporality creates a "discordant concordance" (*Time and Narrative III* 141), or tensive unity, between cosmic and lived time, through which a plot's seemingly linear chronology can represent different appearances of time. Within the narrative temporality of human time, an event that is depicted as "past" or "present" in a plot doesn't necessarily correspond to the "before" or "after" of the episodic structure. In addition, human time can extend the time of events that may have occurred in a short period of time or shorten the time devoted to more drawn out incidents and can connect events that are chronologically separated. For example, *Still Mine* begins with a culminating event, a foreshortened courtroom scene to which it will later return, moves back in time to recount Craig's previous memories of a game that occurred years earlier in his childhood, then returns to the "present" of the episodic structure of the film to portray an incident at a picnic that took place before the initial courtroom scene. These "changes in the tempo, [order,] and duration of scenes create a temporality that is 'lived' in the story that does not coincide with either the chronological time of the world in which the story is [seen], nor the time that the unfolding events are said to depict" (Atkins, "Paul Ricoeur"). Yet, Ricoeur argues, it is this reconfigured temporality that forges a causal continuity between events, both endowing them with necessity and connecting them into a conceptual unity that gives them narrative credibility.

A THICKENING PRESENT

By uniting and rearranging both cosmological and phenomenological (world and lived) time into an intelligible story through the devices of narrative emplotment, human time also enables the construction of what Ricoeur calls a bridge between the past and the present in which the temporal distance separating "then" from "now" is no longer a "dead interval" but becomes a space "generative of meaning" (*Time and Narrative III* 221). We can see how this bridge functions when Craig and Irene's grandson runs off yelling, "We're even!" after his clever riposte to Craig's question about Babe Ruth and, looking at Craig, Irene says how much their grandson reminds her of him. At this point, the camera leaves Craig and Irene and pans around the picnic, stopping to focus on children, spouses, babies – the various generations of their family. Although this scene may seem superfluous to the story, it functions to locate Craig and Irene, and their seven children and their families, in a succession of generations that spans both cosmic and lived time. For although generations are literally connected biologically, argues Ricoeur, it is the generational tie of the family tree that allows us to hold "the thread of life" together and give it meaning (*Memory, History, Forgetting* 379), to make the time of raw life human.

When the concept of generations is used as an intermediary between world or public time and lived private time, what Ricoeur sees as the distancing effect of historical narrative is undone and the relationships among generations become open to reinterpretation. For instance, when Craig talks to his grandson about Babe Ruth or when any elder tells a younger relative of events concerning people he could never have known, Ricoeur interprets such encounters as a partial overlapping between public history and private memory that constitutes a new kind of time, "halfway between private and public time" (*Time and Narrative III* 114). In this new time, the boundary separating historical memory from individual memory is porous, allowing an ancestor's desires, expectations, fears, and memories to intersect with a descendant's, and the hopes, projects, and questions of youth to impact the accustomed certainties of elders. A connection is made between history and the present that, by letting us both revisit our own past experience and share in the experiences of a generation other than our own (*Memory, History, Forgetting* 394), makes history a "we-relationship" through an interlacing chain of memories often called tradition (*Time and Narrative III* 114). Ultimately, it is this relationship that undermines and fractures "historical determinism by retrospectively reintroducing contingency into history" (*Memory, History, Forgetting* 382), leaving us with an appreciation that "what happened is not fixed once and for all," since the facts of events can always be recounted and interpreted otherwise (381).

In their portrayal of the routines of Craig and Irene's daily life, the following scenes present the embodied effects of the "we-relationship" between the past and the present. We first see Irene weeding a garden of raised beds planted in the carcasses of old freezers while Craig nonchalantly walks naked outside to shower, a practice, he tells Irene, that has caused their oldest daughter to think they look like trailer trash. We then learn that Craig has a herd of cows, a field of strawberries, and a wood shop and sawmill where, after felling his own trees, he mills the lumber to build his projects. In these scenes, Craig is portrayed as a capable farmer and jack-of-many-trades who, though relatively unconcerned with appearances, has a certain way of doing things that is at once his own and drawn from his father's tradition. Although these characteristics might make him appear old-fashioned, his actions and demeanour illustrate what Ricoeur described as the effects of duration, or the evidence that "something persists in change" (*Time and Narrative III* 29), and that tradition is not a lifeless "deposit of the past" (238). Since duration, according to Ricoeur, fuses the past with the present, it destabilises the serial succession of nows that marks objective time. As does the incorporation of generational memories, intentions, or expectations into our lives, this fusion thickens the present and makes it dense. This thickened present, then, is no longer simply a moment that passes and disappears, but becomes "the actualization of the future of what is remembered" (35-36), evidence of the prolongation of the past into the present and the future. By weaving together past, present, and future – memory, action, and expectation – the thickened present not only affects the character of our daily lives but strengthens the "we-relationship" by colouring memory anew in light of the completion of its desire.

We also see the effects of duration in the portrayal of Craig and Irene's relationship – in the way they hold hands at the funeral after the picnic or in the way she lies in his arm as the alarm sounds in the morning. When Irene says to Craig, "Take off your clothes, old man," and they embrace and make love, or when she teases him about Bernice, dead for thirty years, declaring she would leave him still if he cheated, or when they recall the drive to St. John and how prim and proper she was until they met, each present moment is expanded through the inclusion of their memories of earlier moments of passion. This effect is particularly evident in the scene in which they reminisce about how he threw up on her sister the night they met. Although separated – he at home and she in hospital rehab – we see their faces, each alone and lonely in the middle of the night, while a voiceover relates the familiar tale of their serendipitous meeting. The paradoxical nature of the absent-presence of these "billows of memories continually rising in the midst of the action" (132) causes time to slow down and creates a multitude of what Ricoeur calls quasi-presents, virtual presents full of recollections and expectations that invade the present moment to shape the actual now (108).

A Dynamic Identity

The way the past intertwines with the present also becomes apparent as Craig and Irene's settled life begins to be troubled by signs attributed to ageing, first revealed by Irene's occasional lapses of memory. When she sees their cows in the road and wonders to whom they belong, unintentionally leaves an oven mitt on the hot stove causing the house to fill with smoke, or slips in and out of the moment while playing cards with friends, although Craig's reactions range from silence to momentary anger, his struggle with how to change their life in order to preserve it becomes visible. This struggle illustrates well Ricoeur's description of narrative identity. In contrast to John Locke's assertion that personal "identity equals sameness with self" throughout life (*Memory, History, Forgetting* 104) and is considered defective whenever conscious and continuous memory of one's actions becomes compromised, Ricoeur argues for a self whose structure rests on the temporal nature of a "dynamic identity" (*Time and Narrative III* 246). For Ricoeur, self-sameness is constituted by all the stories, truthful or fictional, that someone tells about herself or himself and that are used to reconfigure not only the self but even the memory of that self whenever it comes into contact with the present moment. Although this self, admits Ricoeur, cannot remain formally identical to itself in any abstract sense throughout the course of a life, it is nevertheless self-constant in that it "can include change within the cohesion of one lifetime" (246).

In light of Ricoeur's notion of narrative identity, Craig's decision to get rid of the cows and to stop growing strawberries appears to be due less to the endless demands of caring for cattle or to an inability to keep up with the changing regulations regarding the commercial transport of strawberries than to the initial stirrings of an attempt to restructure their identity in a way that will make sense of his life with Irene in the present circumstances. As the film speeds up time with shots of the seasons changing in rapid succession to winter, Craig tells Irene that the water in the toilet froze, that they've already been through three cords of wood, and that it "may not be much longer before this place won't work for us anymore." When Irene responds by declaring that she's "not moving into town" and that he'll have to shoot her before he finds her in a retirement home, Craig tries to assuage her anger – and her fear – by saying that he's thinking of building them a smaller, one-level house. His decision to build reflects not only his refusal of a narrative that would interpret Irene's increasing forgetfulness and inflexibility as a sign of a concomitant decrease in her ability to remain involved in life but his determination to adjust the world around her in a way that will "fit" her changing story and self and allow her to remain fully "human." Now that he has more time, he says, he can do the work himself. "We won't move," he adds, "until we have to."

Unswayed by the reservations of two of their children, who question his ability to continue to care for their mother alone and jokingly wonder if his plans to build won't end up with him injured in a "fit of geriatric stupidity," he forges ahead with the project. When his friend, Chester, who takes a more conventional view of ageing and believes that no man over seventy should ever be on a ladder, asks him if he has a building permit, Craig even tries to comply with what he sees as intrusive new building regulations. Despite his confidence in his ability to construct a sound house, revealed to us in the measured tone with which he lectures the young building inspector on the finer points of lumber and construction he learned from his shipwright father, he finds himself forced to deal with a bureaucracy that will not yield an inch to the length and depth of his experience. Craig's escalating frustration with what he sees as burdensome bureaucratic changes reveals the irony of interpreting those changes that occur as an institution "ages" as signs of progress and increasing competence while regarding those that occur as a human ages as signs of decline and decreasing competence. By the time he returns home one evening to find Irene lying unconscious at the bottom of the stairs, we see the effects of this frustration as he falters and starts to worry that their "luck is beginning to run out." Yet, when Irene wakes up and remembers her fall, she counters his concern about the end of their luck, saying that they must be quite lucky instead, since by all rights she should have broken her hip! Smiling ruefully at her pluck and regaining his customary "nonbureaucratic" resilience, he leaves her with a kiss, off to buy groceries, learn to cook, and rearrange the house so that they can avoid the stairs by moving the bed into the living room and a porta-potty leftover from a recent wedding to the front porch.

Despite Craig's stubborn self-reliance when confronted with all the alterations in his life and his taciturn refusal to fall into what Ricoeur calls the first great trap of old age, sadness at reminders of our mortality (Ricoeur, "Memory, History, Forgiveness" 20), he must choose how to respond, how to continue his story. As Ricoeur explains, this choice first involves recognition of the "existential" fact of our finitude, a fact that cannot be unbound from the philosophical project of ontology – an "analysis which describes the fundamental structure which distinguishes human being from any other kind of being" (Vanhoozer 31) – nor from the quest for meaning in our lives. This choice then involves an awareness that our existential choice takes place in the context of a vast array of "existentiell" responses, or concrete choices about how to live in the world (*Time and Narrative III* 136), actual choices "of certain possibilities [of] involvement in the world" (Vanhoozer 31) that are based on attitudes toward mortality that range from "an anticipatory resoluteness in the face of death" to a more insouciant "celebration of life" (32). These existentiell choices, says Ricoeur, concern both our ethical commitment to others and the use to which we put our talents and abilities (*Time and Narrative III* 64) yet are limited by our condition of being "thrown" into the world at a time and in a constantly-changing set of cultural and social conditions that are not of our choosing. Both the choices and the limits on these choices are produced through what Ricoeur calls institutionalization, a dynamic process that "oscillates between the production of meaning and the production of constraints" on what meanings are permitted or forbidden (*Memory, History, Forgetting* 220) and that is experienced as an unfolding "set of rebellious or docile permissions or obstacles" to action (*Time and Narrative III* 231). It is in the space between the endpoints of the oscillating process of institutionalization and between the existential desire for abstract meaning and the existentiell necessity of concrete choice, Ricoeur concludes, that we have the freedom both to construct our own imaginative variations about how to respond to our twofold experience of time and to do so in a way that reminds us of our connection to others and of the contingency of our ideas and norms (136).

Seen through the lens of Ricoeur's interpretation of the binary character of existence and the dual nature of time, we begin to understand the extent of the difficulty that Craig experiences in deciding how to act. The existential reality of Irene's increasing forgetfulness, realised in his fear of what could happen to her if she were to wander away and in her growing fear of forgetting everything, along with the physical and material demands of the care he must continually exercise to keep track of her, embodied in the aches and fatigue he feels due to his exertions, remind him all too often of the fragility not only of life but of the coherence of the story of their life. In addition, the concerns of his children, such as his daughter's well-meant suggestion that he investigate programs designed to deal with memory loss or his son's comment that strength of character may not be all he needs to complete the project, along with the cavalier unconcern of the bureaucratic state, remind him of the fact that all these events are happening in a cultural context where the ability, and even the right, of the ageing and the old to continue narrating their own lives can be called into question. With all the existential and existentiell constraints hemming him in, it's a daunting task to find a way to respond that will allow him to attest to both his capabilities and his vulnerabilities (*Memory, History, Forgetting* 132, 392) – to choose according to what Heidegger calls his "ownmost possibilities" (*Time and Narrative III* 68) – yet maintain a consistent sense of self and story.

TIME AND THE TRACE

When, within a short span of filmic time, Irene trips over a shoe, actually breaks her hip, and will need weeks of therapy in rehab before she can return home, and Craig is served papers requiring him to appear in court due to his repeated failure to comply with the stop-work order on his house, he begins to wonder if "this may be the start of [his] slow decline." One evening, we see him alone, lines of discouragement framing his face as he holds reams of court papers in one hand while he rests the other on the dining room table. Lost in thought, the camera leaves his face and slowly slides along the nicked and scarred surface of that table. It finally stops on Craig's equally marked hand, focusing in as he gently caresses every dent and scratch. Although Craig does not speak, through a reconfiguration of time, we hear his voice ask Irene if she remembers when he built their dining room table. From the hospital room where she is recovering, her wistful face fills the screen and her voice answers, "We'd been using the sawhorses and planks for so many years, I'd almost given up on getting a proper one."

"My father helped me mill the boards. I put twelve coats of finish on that table."
"It didn't help when Ruth spilled ink on it!"
"I wasn't that upset."
"Oh – you were very table-proud back then."
"The first few years, every nick that table absorbed, I took it personally. It's all I could see. The dent from a fork, the scratch from a skate blade, the ghost of someone's handwriting pressed through a single piece of paper."
"I forgot about that."
"Well, there were a lot of times I regretted not making that table out of oak. But, as the years went by and the scars added up, the imperfections turned that table into something else. That's the thing about pine – holds a lot of memories."

Perhaps, more than any other, this scene illustrates Ricoeur's theories about how we make sense of the past and our ongoing involvement with it through memory, despite the irresolvable contradictions of time. Although Craig remains seated at the table, prompted by the traces of the past inscribed in its surface in the form of literal tracks documenting events in his children's lives, and by a remembered past or imagined future conversation with Irene, he immerses himself in memory. This immersion or journey through time, argues Ricoeur, lies at the heart of the question about the relationship of the past to the present. Since the trace is present to us, how, asks Ricoeur, "is it that such an inscription is itself present and yet also a sign of what is not present, of what existed previously?" (*Memory, History, Forgetting* 425). How can this present-absence lead us now to where we are no longer? Similar to the markings on the table where each dent or mark of absence records a past action on a table that endures and is, therefore, both absent and present, the trace embodies "a sign of its absent cause"; the trace, continues Ricoeur, must be a sign of the "passage of memory from the virtual to the actual" as well (436).

Drawing from Bergson's *Matter and Memory*, Ricoeur further proposes that, in order for us to remember anything, "something of the original impression has to have remained" (430) as an image that has survived. Whenever we encounter a memory, whether through recognition or what Ricoeur describes as the happy coincidence of discovering something again, or through recollection or what Ricoeur calls the work of searching for a memory, we must assume that it was, in principle, always available, inscribed on our minds and waiting, if not always accessible to us (433). The continuous survival of the past in memory, says Ricoeur, drawing again from Bergson and Deleuze in Deleuze's *Bergsonism*, presents a profound paradox concerning time: that "the past is 'contemporaneous' with the present that it *has been* [and that] *all* our past coexists with each present" (434). Memories, argues Ricoeur, whether we are conscious of them or not, must therefore have the same kind of existence as do the objects in the world around us when we are not perceiving them. When unperceived, objects are latent and powerless, unless we, through either chance or an act of will, come into contact with them and incorporate them into our active perception. As for memories, they also remain latent until we, through the process of recognition or recollection, "leap outside the circle traced around us by our attention to life into the region of dreams beyond the realm of action" (435) and "grasp the past again in the present" (436). Once grasped, a memory passes from its virtual state to the actual and tends to imitate perception, becoming able to reinsert itself "within the thickness of lived action" (439). Yet, at the same time, it "remains attached to the past by its deepest roots" (439). Consequently, concludes Ricoeur, the trace is a sign of the self-survival of memories "contemporaneous with the original experience" (440) and extends an invitation to us to explore this self-surviving "mass of marks designating what we have seen, heard, felt, learned, acquired" both throughout our individual lives and in our interactions with others (441).

For Craig, the traces in the table and his meditation on the memories and history they embody lead him to revisit the past, not to see it as passed and dead but in order to rethink "what was once thought," to reacquaint himself with unrealised dreams (380). It is there, in that moment, that his decision to build a new house in that particular spot with a view that Irene always loved makes sense. Although we, the audience, are never made fully aware of the circumstances that might have prevented him from realizing his dream earlier, we see in his decision to continue building, despite the potential consequences of ignoring the stop-work order, a determination to open up "aborted potentialities in the supposedly closed past" (*Time and Narrative III* 227). By returning to a moment of the past when "the future was not yet decided, where the past was itself a space of experience open to a horizon of expectation" (227), he frees himself to refashion both their stories and their selves in a way that will fit their new circumstances. He also begins to recognise that the passage of time and the scars and imperfections left by its passing *are* the content of our story, the stuff out of which we construct our life and our identity. Since time "needs a body in order to externalize itself, to make itself visible" (138), age, known through the traces inscribed on our hearts, minds, and bodies and on the objects among which we live, is the only evidence we have of our passage through life. If we, as Craig once wished for the table, were to become impervious to the marks of time, marks that we often see as imperfections, we would have no memory, no story, and no self. These scars and imperfections are what make us human and what enable us to tell our story in human time.

THE RESOURCE OF FORGETTING

Rather than fall prey to the cultural narrative of decline that, given its emphasis on loss and approaching death, would preclude his ability to dream and to act, Craig's immersion in the past permits him to grasp the possibility of reimagining and reconstructing a future inspired by hope. Incorporated into this decision is his refusal to see Irene's lapses of memory as nothing but loss. When he responds to her fear that she might forget everything by saying, "So what! We're still here; we have each other," and by telling her she will still be his Irene, he is affirming their right to continue narrating their story even in the absence of their "prologue," their years together that have led to this present. In this context, the word "still" harkens back to Ricoeur's concept of duration or to the persistence of something throughout change and to his definition of self-constancy or a kind of self-sameness that is inclusive of change. That this change might include memory loss does not obviate Ricoeur's point. Memory, argues Ricoeur, is most often defined "as a struggle against forgetting." Yet, "the specter of a memory that would never forget anything" would be considered monstrous (*Memory, History, Forgetting* 413). In light of this paradox, Ricoeur asks, "is forgetting itself a dysfunction," a definitive erasure of traces (416), or is forgetting a reserve, "one of the conditions for [memory]" itself (426)?

The neurosciences, argues Ricoeur, approach the subject of forgetting only in the context of dysfunction and distortion. Forgetting is seen as an existential threat against which "we conduct the work of memory in order to slow its course, even hold it at bay" (426). Deplored, as are ageing and death, forgetting is associated with the inevitable and irremediable erasure of traces and with mortality. Neuroscientific research seeks correlations between structure and function in order to delay this erasure through understanding the objective, biological basis of memory and forgetting. But, Ricoeur asks, were the work of correlation complete, would the neuroscientific knowledge gained bring us any closer to the subjective, phenomenological significance of memory and forgetting? For forgetting is intimately bound up with memory as well, in the sense that when we remember something, the image comes back to us. Since a memory cannot return without first being lost or forgotten, it had to have survived the forgetting in some form. This form Ricoeur calls "pure memory" (438) and is characterised by its unconscious existence, its latent ability to conserve the traces of our having-been. Pure memory, he continues, is "one of the figures of fundamental forgetting, a reserve or a resource" removed "from the vigilance of consciousness" (440) and experienced as both the daily erosion of memories and as their unexpected return. Forgetting, concludes Ricoeur, is not only an "inexorable destruction" (442) but also an "immemorial resource offered to the work of remembering" (443). In the end, forgetting's work of eroding can be just as significant as its work of maintaining.

Understood in this way, the misfortune of definitive forgetting that Irene so fears demands not only an existentiell or practical response that seeks to delay or remediate any physical causes of her increasing forgetfulness but an existential or personal response that, as Ricoeur writes, "beckons us more to poetry and to wisdom than to science" (427) in the search for what it means to be human. Here again, we return to what Ricoeur calls the poetics of narrative (*Time and Narrative III* 4). Just as narrative can close the gap between lived and cosmic time, reveal how the past and the present are contemporaneous, and narrow the divide between history and fiction, it also can be used to maintain a coherent sense of self and identity by diminishing the distance between memory and forgetting – by making their seeming opposition productive. In light of the coherence that narrative can bestow on life, Craig's insistence on remaining with Irene and caring for her for as long as he is able is a way of maintaining their story, of continuing to live up to death. The wisdom of his decision is reflected in the change in his son's attitude, from the initial sceptical comment, "*Maybe* Dad has it under control; *maybe* he's making the right decision," to his later remark that they'd definitely "need to warm up the hearse" if he were asking for too much help. Although acutely aware of his mortality, Craig is determined not to let the hearse pre-emptively run over "the joy of living to the end" (*Living Up to Death* 11).

MOURNING AND CHEERFULNESS

What Ricoeur would call the "insouciance" or "cheerfulness" that colours Craig's renewed appetite for life (11) is challenged when he learns of Chester's death. Brought to tears by the loss, and possibly by the unresolved anger expressed in their last encounter, kneeling by his bed, we see Craig trying to pray. From her bed in the hospital rehab, we see Irene's tear-stained face and hear her ask, "Since when did you get religion?"

"I figured this was a good time to hedge my bets," answers Craig. "Hoping for a miracle, I suppose."

"I miss you," Irene says.

"I miss you too," he answers and asks how she is.
"I've been better," concedes Irene.
"Me, too," Craig whispers as tears stream down his face.

In this scene, the sense of loss that Craig and Irene feel at their temporary separation is heightened and accentuated by the sudden death of their friend. Craig's inclination to pray as a response to this loss expresses what Ricoeur describes as an attempt to connect with the "Essential" (14). In the face of death, Ricoeur argues, the religious, "which exists culturally only as articulated in the language of a historical religion" or belief (15), transcends the limitations of any particular religion or time to become transcultural. "Because dying is transcultural" (16) this search for the Essential is the experience of loss and mourning, an experience that unites all religions despite their historical context. Ricoeur further explains that the loss of someone close results not only in a separation but is an "amputation of oneself to the extent that the relation with the one who has disappeared forms an integral part of one's identity" (*Memory, History, Forgetting* 359). This loss of self, continues Ricoeur, is a stage in learning to imagine, to anticipate, our own death. And it is within this feeling of anticipation that "the work of mourning begins to take shape" (359). That work, posits Ricoeur, involves separating ourselves from the lost person by transforming "the physical absence of the lost into an inner presence" (366) thus incorporating a part of the lost person into ourselves as an integral part of our story and even our self. The incorporation of the loss occasioned by mourning is what allows us to remember the person; and memory is what enables us to conserve the traces of that person in the immemorial resource of memory-forgetting that underlies the work of remembering. Mourning, Ricoeur concludes, is not something to avoid but is "a part of our reality" since to be alive must "include the absence of what no longer is but once was" (Abel xii). Hence, mourning, as a work of memory, is one way we access the absent-presence of the past to refigure our lives through the creative use of narrative.

At the end of the movie, we return to the courtroom scene with a deeper understanding of the circumstances surrounding the decision Craig has to make and again we hear him ask, "Are you a baseball fan, your honor?" When the judge responds with a puzzled look, Craig, baseball in memory and in hand, explains that he has always appreciated "how you could compare a player in one era to a player in another." Despite any changes in the rules, you could make such comparisons because the traditions of the game endured through the years. It is the same with building, he says. In spite of changes in the religion of rules, the tradition has endured. Apologizing for seeming to put himself above the law, he argues that, despite appearances, he remained true to what is essential about building and that his house is sound. When Irene gets out of the hospital next week, he states, "Either I'm going to jail or I'm going home."

The final scenes, interweaving shots of Craig and Irene at Chester's funeral with shots of them moving into their new home, bring both narrative coherence and closure to the story. Through the use of the techniques of narrative emplotment, the construction of human time, and the development of dynamic narrative identities, we see both the continuity of their lives (in the way that they sit in the same place in the small church and the way that Craig lovingly strokes the worn wood on the top of the pew in front of him) and the changes (in the tears that course unbidden down Craig's face and the fact that Irene is wheelchair-bound rather than standing beside him). The constitutive relationship between death and life, endings and beginnings, is also visible as Craig reluctantly says goodbye to his old house. Nostalgically fingering the marks on the doorframe that document his children's growth as he closes one door, he smiles gleefully as he reads, "No jail for Morrison!" in the newspaper and opens a new door to walk in to a waiting Irene. By juxtaposing scenes of loss with those of gain, *Still Mine* illustrates well what Ricoeur calls "the intimate bond between mourning and cheerfulness" (Abel xiii) in the construction of a cohesive self that inhabits human time.

CONCLUSION

As the screen fades to black once more, we learn that Craig celebrated his ninety-first birthday in the new house with Irene at his side. Although not privy to the actual celebration, we can imagine that it took place, as did Ricoeur's ninetieth, in the company of family and friends and in an atmosphere that expressed, as Ricoeur said, "the simple happiness of still being alive and, above all, the love of life, shared with those I love" (Goldenstein 94). Although Ricoeur never could close the gap between refusal and acceptance of our mortal condition, he concluded that acceptance of death meant not only learning how to die but "learning finally how to live" (*Living Up to Death* 85). And learning how to live, for him, meant recognition of our mutual vulnerability and indebtedness and of our duty to care for each other (*Oneself as Another*). Only by redirecting the desire to live toward others who survive and by bestowing on them the traces of one's life as "gifts" that ask "to be recalled, reopened, rethought" (Abel xxi), said Ricoeur, could life prove to be invulnerable to death and could every life and every death acquire meaning.

In the end, the story told in *Still Mine* provides a better understanding of what Ricoeur meant by the circular relationship between narrative and life. Lived as history, then fictionalised as filmic narrative, *Still Mine* can return to life to the extent that it influences us to reconfigure our lives in light of both a cultural narrative that tends to pre-emptively exclude people who are old from continuing a story and the corporeal limits of human existence. Through mimesis, the three stages of "a movement that originates in culture as a symbolic order, passes into a fixed form, then is reintroduced into the cultural sphere in the consciousness of a [viewer] whose way of being in the world has been altered" by the experience (Dowling 2), the world of this film can intersect with the lived world of the viewer (*Time and Narrative III* 159). And to the extent that this intersection is internalised, it can support what Ricoeur experienced for himself in his last years – an appetite for life that enriches and enlarges, rather than diminishes, our idea of self and story as we grow older. Ricoeur's project of making life intelligible and meaningful through the use of narrative to restructure time and identity, especially when used in conjunction with other resources and research in the field of age studies (a topic for another paper), not only enriches and enlarges our lives but can do the same for the critical study of ageing and old age itself.

"I would have been much happier if I'd just stuck you in an old folk's home," quips Craig's son John. Responding that he was thinking the same thing about John, Craig jokes that they might have been able to get a discount—two for the price of one! "You got another project in mind?" John asks.
"Maybe," Craig answers. "I can't just sit around all day. Time enough for that when I'm dead."

REFERENCES

Abel, Olivier. Preface. *Living Up to Death.* By Paul Ricoeur. Trans. David Pellauer. Chicago: U of Chicago P, 2009. vii-xxiv. Print.

Deleuze, Gilles. *Bergsonism.* Trans. High Tomlinson and Barbara Habberjam. New York: Zone, 2006. Print.

Dowling, William C. *Ricoeur on Time and Narrative.* Notre Dame: U of Notre Dame P, 2011. Print.

Goldenstein, Catherine. Postface. *Living Up to Death.* By Paul Ricoeur. Trans. David Pellauer. Chicago: U of Chicago P, 2009. 91-97. Print.

"Paul Ricoeur." By Kim Atkins. *Internet Encyclopedia of Philosophy.* Web. 2 Aug. 2014.

"Paul Ricoeur." *Stanford Encyclopedia of Philosophy.* 18 Apr. 2011. Web. 1 Aug. 2014.

Ricoeur, Paul. *Living Up to Death.* Trans. David Pellauer. Chicago: U of Chicago P, 2009. Print.

---. *Memory, History, Forgetting.* Trans. Kathleen Blamey and David Pellauer. Chicago: U of Chicago P, 2006. Print.

---. Interview by Sorin Antohi. "Memory, History, Forgiveness: A Dialogue between Paul Ricoeur and Sorin Antohi." Amherst: Trivium Publishers, 2005. Web. 1 Aug. 2014.

---. *Oneself as Another.* Trans. Kathleen Blamey. Chicago: U of Chicago P. 1992. Print.

---. *Time and Narrative.* Vol. 3. Trans. Kathleen Blamey and David Pellauer. Chicago: U of Chicago P, 1990. Print.

Still Mine. Dir. Michael McGowan. Perf. James Cromwell, Genevieve Bujold. Telefilm Canada, 2013. DVD.

Valdes, Mario J., ed. *A Ricoeur Reader: Reflections and Imagination.* Toronto: U of Toronto P, 1991. Print.

Vanhoozer, Kevin J. *Biblical Narrative in the Philosophy of Paul Ricoeur.* Cambridge: Cambridge UP, 1990. Print.

Memory, Dementia, and Narrative Identity in Alice Munro's "The Bear Came Over the Mountain"

Sara Strauss

Introduction

During the last decades science, as well as the humanities and the arts, has paid close attention to the research on human memory, its biological preconditions, and its representation in culture. In cultural studies, the research paradigm of cultural memory (A. Assmann; J. Assmann) has shed light on various methods of commemorating collective experiences through memorials, historical sites, events, or cultural artefacts. In addition to this focus on collective memory, a growing public interest in the memory of individuals manifests itself in the vast amount of recent publications of autobiographical texts and memoirs and their positive reception by the public.[1] As Couser states, "this is an age – if not *the age* – of memoir" (3). It is against the background of an ageing society and age-related diseases which threaten the individual's abilities to remember that the current

---

1   The wide public interest in memoirs is revealed in their high print run as much as in the prevalence of autobiographical texts in the bestseller listings over the last few years. In the *New York Times* bestseller list of May 4, 2014, for example, nine of the fifteen nonfiction books are biographical texts or memoirs ("Best Sellers"). Ben Yagoda observes an increase of sales of memoirs by 400 percent in the USA from 2004 to 2008 (7).

growing interest in memory attains further significance. The relationship between memory and forgetting has a decisive influence on the formation of personal identity. Traces left by earlier activities help people to remember the past and also affect their perspectives on the present and the future as well as on their worldview. A loss of memory due to age-related diseases, such as dementia and Alzheimer's, and the inability to interpret one's own traces can bring about a different perception of an individual's sense of self.

Following this line of thought, the present article applies Paul Ricoeur's concepts of trace and narrative identity to Alice Munro's "The Bear Came Over the Mountain," first published in 1999.[2] Munro's short story depicts the unrelenting progress of dementia in the protagonist Fiona and unveils her husband Grant's confrontation with the cognitive decline of his wife as well as with his private recollections of their past. Grant reflects on his and his wife's shared life and their attempts at coming to terms with Fiona's condition from its onset, through her hospitalisation, to late-stage dementia. The story focuses on Grant's thoughts on his prior unfaithfulness to Fiona and his powerlessness in the advent of mental decay. Munro's narrative, which is told from Grant's point of view, deals with the all-embracing effects of memory loss on the patients' and their relatives' lives and illustrates their struggle to comprehend the changes of behaviour dementia entails. The figural narrator's meditations on traces of his and his wife's lives exemplify the initial denial of the diagnosis and its effects on their lives.

This paper also centres on how Grant's ruminations on his earlier, morally-wanting behaviour stimulate the reader to ethical reflections on moral values, questions of interpersonal relationships, and challenges arising with old age and disease. The narration of memories can lead the narrator and the narratee to new positions on the stories presented whereby, according to Ricoeur, they acquire a renewed narrative identity (246-49). The philosopher describes the process of reading or listening to a narrative as an identity-shaping process through which the recipients attain another

---

2   First published in *The New Yorker*, December 27, 1999. In 2001 the story was anthologised in an extended version in Munro's short story collection *Hateship, Friendship, Courtship, Loveship, Marriage* (2001). All page numbers of the following quotations refer to this anthologised version of the story.

perspective on their self, on life, and the world surrounding them (246, 249). This new perspective can, for example, stimulate ethical considerations on the part of the reader and may result in moral behaviour which is not only led by principles and values but also predominantly by empathy (Hoffman 295). Narrative empathy, "the sharing of feeling and perspective-taking induced by reading, viewing, hearing, or imagining narratives of another's situation and condition" (Keen par. 1), can thus contribute to a change in the readers' attitude, their moral judgements, as well as their actions. This study applies these concepts to the difficult situation of memory loss caused by dementia, analyses how the protagonists' traces surface in Alice Munro's short story and elaborates on the readers' possible processes of forming a narrative identity.

ALICE MUNRO'S DEMENTIA NARRATIVE AND PAUL RICOEUR'S TRACE

Ricoeur borrows Littré's definition of "trace" as a "vestige that a human being or an animal has left on the place where it passed," or in a very general sense "any mark left by a thing." In this general use of the term Ricoeur observes the paradox that,

[o]n the one hand, the trace is visible here and now, as a vestige, a mark. On the other hand, there is a trace (or track) because 'earlier' a human being or an animal passed this way. [...] [O]nce the passage has taken place, the past falls behind. It passed this way. And we say that time itself passes. Where then is the paradox? In the fact that the passage no longer is but the trace remains. (119)

Applying this conception of the trace to the topic of dementia and memory loss, the trace can lead back to an activity which the sufferer of dementia performed earlier yet cannot remember in his or her present condition of failing mental capacity. The trace, therefore, becomes the track to a prior existence of the patients which might cause them to remember their experience or can help their relatives and caretakers to draw conclusions about their prior life:

The trace invites us to pursue it, to follow it back, if possible to the person or animal who passed this way. We may lose the trail. It may even disappear or lead nowhere. The trace can be wiped out, for it is fragile and needs to be preserved intact; otherwise, the passage did occur but it did not leave a trace, it simply happened. (120)

In the same way as Ricoeur stresses the fragility of the trace in general, a trace can also be wiped out and its trail can get lost due to dementia. If a person suffering from dementia is no longer able to pursue his or her own trace, then the memory of his or her past activities is lost.

The paradoxical facet of the trace increases the psychological and emotional disturbance of sufferers and their relatives. Ricoeur emphasises "the strangeness of the trace which 'is not a sign like others', inasmuch as it is always a passage that it indicates, not some possible presence" (125). The paradox described by Ricoeur that "the passage no longer is but the trace remains" (119) makes it difficult for relatives and caretakers of sufferers of dementia to come to terms with the disease. The recovery of the past through the interpretation of traces gives evidence of the discrepancy between the present condition and a healthy past and is therefore an endeavour that arouses the relatives' emotions. Relatives and caretakers are witnesses to the traces of the patients' earlier, healthy life, for example through the physically robust body of early-onset patients or through documents of their lives, such as photos, written documents, their works, etc. They also bear witness to the patients' change of cognitive abilities, character traits, and behaviour. The paradox which the patients' relatives experience is that, at first, physically the individuals suffering from dementia and the traces they left behind remain unaltered. Nonetheless, the patient's mental abilities turn them into strangers who can no longer retrieve their past actions or what Ricoeur calls "the passage." It is this aspect of age-related mental diseases which makes it difficult for relatives to comprehend the symptoms of the disease.

In Alice Munro's short story "The Bear Came Over the Mountain" Fiona's mental deterioration soon leaves her unable to remember her prior actions and Grant endeavours to perceive traces of his wife's former self and their shared life. In the early stages of Fiona's disease, although she continually forgets recent events, Fiona still shows her usual self: she has not lost her sense of humour, can laugh at herself, and is quick at making decisions. Grant remembers incidents of their shared life that take the shape of a trace as the moment when Fiona proposed marriage to him. This trace brings back to Grant memories of past traits of his wife: "She had the spark of life" (276). A year after becoming aware of her cognitive decline, Fiona moves to the nursing home Meadowlake while she is still fully conscious of the fact that she is making a life-changing decision. On the day when Grant takes Fiona to the nursing home, he observes his wife's ageing body, which is still "upright and trim" (276), and recognises in it all the traces of the young woman he fell in love with: "She looked just like herself on this day" (277). For Grant, Fiona's healthy physical appearance at this late stage in life functions as a trace of her past mental health. It displays various habits and features that are characteristic of Fiona's identity: her graceful body from her habit of skiing and long walks in the countryside, her long hair is a reminder of Fiona's and her mother's political attitude and their nonconformity. On her way to the nursing home Fiona still sticks to her habit of emphasising her lips with red lipstick before leaving the house. Munro's recurring theme of "the degree to which an individual's present is a fabric woven from the past" (Hooper x) continuously surfaces in her depiction of the protagonist. The traces of Fiona's past healthy life and the fact that her outward appearance has not been altered make it difficult however for her husband to comprehend that it is her mind which is changing and to accept his wife's mental deterioration, gradually being revealed in the course of her illness:

> She went to town and phoned him from a booth to ask him how to drive home. She went for her walk across the field into the woods and came home by the fence line – a very long way round. She said that she'd counted on fences always taking you somewhere. (277)

Fiona uses the expression "counted on" and resorts to the received wisdom that "fences always tak[e] you somewhere" in order to explain her detour. Munro here presents a common strategy of dementia patients to conceal their memory failure but also to continue taking part in conversations fluently and to regain self-confidence by reverting to idioms, fixed expressions, formulaic phrases, or general truths that explain their behaviour or make up for a loss of words (Davis and Maclagan 102). The patients' strategies of concealing, trivialising, or ridiculing their failing cognitive functions cover up the severity of the condition. In relation to this episode, Grant states:

> It was hard to figure out. She said that about fences as if it was a joke, and she had remembered the phone number without any trouble.
> "I don't think it's anything to worry about," she said. "I expect I'm just losing my mind." (278)

In the same way in which Fiona first manages to delude Grant, she also deceives a policeman who picks her up on the street:

> Fiona, who no longer went shopping alone, disappeared from the supermarket while Grant had his back turned. A policeman picked her up as she walked down the middle of the road, blocks away. He asked her name and she answered readily. Then he asked her the name of the prime minister of the country.
> "If you don't know that, young man, you really shouldn't be in such a responsible job." He laughed. (279)

By joking and employing irony Fiona trivialises her memory loss and thereby makes it difficult for her husband and other people to grasp the truth of her real condition. However, the yellow notes that Fiona leaves everywhere in her house reveal how she gradually acknowledges her cognitive problems. Having forgotten about the contents of cupboards and drawers, she attaches little notes to them which inform about their contents. Grant, still unaware of Fiona's disturbed state of mind, wonders about the purpose of these notes:

> Over a year ago, Grant had started noticing so many little yellow notes stuck up all over the house. [...] The new notes were different [from those before]. Taped onto the kitchen drawers – Cutlery, Dishtowels, Knives. Couldn't she have just opened the drawers and seen what was inside? (277)

The yellow notes form a document of Fiona's mental deterioration. As such they "function[ ] as a trace of the past" (Ricoeur 118) and evidence the moment when Fiona admitted her problems to herself. For the protagonist the little notes are traces of her former self and serve as documents to remind her of her previous agile mental activity. Though Grant is at first confused by the notes, he is later able to interpret them as traces of Fiona's realisation of her fading mental faculties.

When Grant is finally confronted with the doctor's diagnosis that Fiona's memory loss "might be selective at first" (278), he questions its accuracy and tries to close his eyes to reality: "'She's always been a bit like this,' Grant said to the doctor. [...] He tried without success to explain something more – to explain how Fiona's surprise and apologies about all this seemed somehow like routine courtesy, not quite concealing a private amusement" (278). Like Munro's other stories, whose "overarching point" Hooper considers to be "character analysis" (x), "The Bear Came Over the Mountain" seeks "to capture and delineate the essence of character" (viii). By internal focalisation through Grant and by direct, indirect, and free indirect style the narrative discloses his intimate thoughts. Grant's refusal to accept the irretrievability of their past life becomes obvious in his reflections, his doubts about his wife's diagnosis, his disbelief in the truth, and his hope beyond reason. Fiona's random remembrance of past experiences complicates Grant's conflict about coming to terms with his wife's changing mental capacity. As they both drive to the nursing home for her hospitalisation, a hollow which has completely frozen over reminds both of them of their past habit of skiing at night. Alice Munro here represents Grant's thoughts in free indirect style: "So if she could remember that so vividly and correctly, could there really be so much the matter with her?" (280). Grant's intimate reflections reveal his doubts and his adherence to the unrealistic hope that they could retrieve their situation of being a healthy married couple.

NARRATIVE IDENTITIES AND ETHICS IN ALICE MUNRO'S DEMENTIA NARRATIVE

In *Time and Narrative* Ricoeur points to the strong ethical function that narratives perform:

The plea that the theory of narrative can always oppose to ethics' claim to be the sole judge of the constitution of subjectivity would be to recall that narrativity is not denuded of every normative, evaluative, or prescriptive dimension. The theory of reading has warned us that the strategy of persuasion undertaken by the narrator is aimed at imposing on the reader a vision of the world that is never ethically neutral, but that rather implicitly or explicitly induces a new evaluation of the world and of the reader as well. In this sense, narrative already belongs to the ethical field in virtue of its claim – inseparable from its narration – to ethical justice. (249)

As the philosopher elaborates, the reception of a story always "induces a new evaluation of the world" on the part of the reader. As a result of the reader's perception of the plot and of the character's traits and moral values presented in a narrative, he or she reflects on the narrator's "vision of the world" and on his or her own. In this process of reading or listening to a story, readers develop a narrative identity. That is, through the use of their imagination they engage in "a thought experiment by means of which [they] try to inhabit worlds foreign to [them]" (249). By plunging themselves into the storyworld, the readers gain experiences that differ from their own situation but that they may apply to the real world. For example, narratives may present topographical, political, or social circumstances that differ from the readers'. They can depict models for actions as well as fictional characters that act as role models or antiheros for the reader. As a result of the transposition of the perceived experience to the real world, the readers are empowered to attain new perspectives on the world they live in, on their selves and their actions. They can thereby further develop their individual identity:

This process of emplotment [...] offers practical proposals for living, prescriptions *for* identity which when taken up become constitutive *of* one's own identity through the deliberation of decision, the commitment of choice, and the initiative of action. What narratives offer are imaginary linguistic models or configurations for living that become identifiable with who we are through the reconnection of narrative and life, that is, through the refiguring reconnection of the world of the text to the world of the reader. (Venema 240)

Narratives inspire the readers' imagination, immerse them in other worlds, and indicate different choices for alternative actions that can be transferred to the readers' real environment. According to Ricoeur, "[t]his is when reading becomes a provocation to be and to act differently" (249). By perceiving and imagining plots, characters, and actions that may correspond to or differ from the readers' own experiences, their own behaviour, opinion, or morals, the recipients are encouraged to reflection and can attain a critical stance with which they can refigure their own behaviour. As Keen remarks, "when readers' attitudes alter, or when they receive tacit or explicit encouragement to undertake altruistic action on behalf of represented others for whom they feel narrative empathy, the impact can be considered an aspect of ethics in narrative discourse" (par. 11).

There is, hence, a strong connection between the development of the readers' narrative identities through reading a text and the formation of their personal and ethical principles. In this way, the reception of narratives can inspire readers to moral judgements and motivate their ethical commitment. The readers transform and develop their own identity by applying the principles and values or the models for action presented in the narrative to their own life. This process of refiguring and adapting the narrative and of giving new meaning to it can initiate a change in the reader's actions. In brief, Ricoeur considers that narrative identity is "the poetic resolution of the hermeneutic circle" (248). To Ricoeur, identity is not

> understood in the sense of being the same (*idem*), [but] identity understood in the sense of oneself as self-same [*soi-même*] (*ipse*). [...] Self-sameness, 'self-constancy,' can escape the dilemma of the Same and the Other to the extent that its identity rests on a temporal structure that conforms to the model of dynamic identity arising from the poetic composition of a narrative text. The self characterized by self-sameness may then be said to be refigured by the reflective application of such narrative configurations. (246)

When defining identity as self-sameness, the philosopher highlights the continual development of a person's or a community's identity through time, and he asserts that "this narrative identity, constitutive of self-constancy, can include change, mutability, within the cohesion of one lifetime" (246). Just as a person's identity changes over the person's lifetime "narrative identity is not a stable and seamless identity. [...] [I]t is always possible to weave different, even opposed, plots about our lives"

(248). While the identity of one reader differs at different stages of his or her life, naturally the narrative identity of one reader differs from the narrative identity of another reader, as do the individual experiences, moral values and principles that guide their actions. As Venema points out, "there is no meta-narrative that can totalize experience. Narrative identity is an identity of plurality, of many stories" (241).

The way in which Munro's short story induces the reader to ethical reflection and to the formation of a narrative identity will be detailed in the following paragraphs. Beyond ethical considerations with regard to the special situation of elderly people suffering from age-related diseases, such as dementia and Alzheimer's, Munro's story elicits thoughts on values such as faithfulness and altruism. It is primarily the insight into Grant's inner life, especially the absence of any genuine repentance for his adultery and his infidelity to Fiona, and his unusual behaviour that oscillates between altruism and egotism when his wife, due to dementia, does not recognise him anymore, which engages the reader in ethical considerations of the "vision of the world" (Ricoeur 249) presented in "The Bear Came Over the Mountain."

Despite his dedication to Fiona once she is affected by dementia, Grant's memories of his past extramarital affairs reveal that he is, in Héliane Ventura's words, "a narcissistic and egomaniac philanderer" (par. 18). During the first four weeks of Fiona's stay in Meadowlake, when Grant is not permitted to visit his wife, he is haunted by a nightmare that one of his love affairs might be made public. His adultery has left traces on Grant's subconscious which surface in his nightmare. In his dream a colleague advises Grant: "'I wouldn't laugh,' he said to Grant, who did not think he had been laughing. 'And if I were you I'd try to prepare Fiona.'" (285). Although the fact that Grant is haunted by a nightmare reveals his feeling of guilt about betraying his wife, his intimate thoughts upon waking show that Grant does not repent of his infidelity. Instead, he plays down his behaviour through comparison with another husband's unfaithfulness: "The colleague was one of those husbands and fathers who had been among the first to throw away their neckties and leave home to spend every night on a floor mattress with a bewitching young mistress" (284). Grant's memories of his immoral behaviour bear a strong sense of self-justification. Even when confronted with the bewildering experience of Fiona's dementia and her need for help, Grant does not show genuine repentance for deceiving his wife. Beyond trivialising his own secret betrayal of Fiona against other men's instant divorces from their wives, Grant recalls what he considers to have been "acts of kindness and generosity and even sacrifice" towards the women he had affairs with:

> Nowhere was there any acknowledgment that the life of a philanderer (if that was what Grant had to call himself – he who had not had half as many conquests or complications as the man who had reproached him in his dream) involved acts of kindness and generosity and even sacrifice. [...] Many times he had catered to a woman's pride, to her fragility, by offering more affection – or a rougher passion – than anything he really felt. (286)

Munro here satirises Grant's narcissism and self-absorption. Through free indirect style the author discloses the protagonist's attempts to whitewash and justify his behaviour which implies a distancing effect on the reader who sees through Grant's self-centredness and his lack of repentance in the face of Fiona's fatal disease.

As a result of this moral distance from the protagonist and figural narrator, the reader develops a narrative identity that differs from Grant's one-dimensional point of view. Due to the initial focus of Munro's story on Fiona's disease and her courageous, even self-ironic acceptance of her fate, the reader feels empathy with Fiona and condemns Grant's egotism. Against the background of the indignities dementia causes Fiona to experience day after day, the reader understands that a respectful interpersonal relationship is of the highest moral value. Yet there is a multiplicity of interpretations readers can ascribe to the story and which will affect their "vision of the world" (Ricoeur 249). As already noted above, the readers' narrative identities, shaped by the contemplations or lessons transferred from the fictional world to their real life, differ depending on the individual reader's frame of reference, for example their personality, personal experiences, moral values, religious beliefs, social and political attitudes. Consequently Ricoeur emphasises, "it is always possible to weave different, even opposed, plots about our lives" (248). In this regard, Munro knowingly leaves her short story ambiguous. In the ensuing plot twist she puts traditional concepts of moral values to the test. When Grant is finally allowed to visit Fiona in the nursing home, she neither remembers him nor their marriage. Instead, Fiona shows deep affection for another patient, Aubrey. As Jonathan Franzen asserts, "it's only now, for the first time, that the old betrayer is being betrayed. And does Grant finally come to regret those affairs? Well, no, not at all." During the following months Grant experiences what it means to be an outsider and an intruder on Fiona's and Aubrey's life at Meadowlake. When Aubrey is released from the temporary care at Meadowlake and returns home to his wife, Fiona is so severely emotionally disturbed that her mental condition affects her physical health. In an effort to prevent Fiona from being relocated to the second floor of the nursing home, which "he had thought [...] was for people whose minds were disturbed" (309), Grant persuades Marian, Aubrey's wife, to bring her husband back. Grant's efforts to ensure his wife's emotional wellbeing can be considered ambiguous. On the one hand, Grant selflessly encourages his wife's attachment to another man for the sake of her emotional and physical comfort. On the other hand, traces of Grant's prior infidelity towards his wife surface and Munro hints at Grant's return to his habit of extramarital affairs. Whereas Grant's flirtation with Marian can at first sight be interpreted as a selfless means to bring Aubrey back to Fiona, Grant's intimate thoughts presented in free indirect style reveal the erotic attraction he feels for the woman. What he mainly remembers from his first encounter with Marian in the parking lot at Meadowlake are her "trim waist and wide buttocks" (310). His thoughts during their first conversation when he visits her at her house divert to Marian's "[w]rinkled neck, youthfully full and up-tilted breasts" (314). On his way home Grant imagines how his life might have differed if, instead of the intellectual Fiona, he had married the pragmatic Marian (318-19). At the same time, he is relieved that he has not "stayed where he belonged" (318) but married Fiona. Grant's inner ruminations once again reveal the contradictions between his behaviour and his private thoughts. As McGill states, Munro "tinges Grant's generosity with a whiff of egoism, as when he privately enters into a not-entirely-indifferent appraisal of Marian's physical attributes. Consequently, his claim to be pursuing 'fine, generous schemes' carries a certain irony" (100). It is Munro's use of irony and her narrative techniques of internal focalisation and free indirect style which give an ambiguous view of Grant's (im)moral behaviour:

For instance, if he wanted to, would he be able to break her [Marian] down, get her to the point where she might listen to him about taking Aubrey back to Fiona? [...] Where could that tremor lead them? To an upset, to the end of her self-preservation? To Fiona's happiness?
It would be a challenge. A challenge and a creditable feat. Also a joke that could never be confided to anybody – to think that by his bad behaviour he'd be doing good for Fiona. (320)

As a result of Munro's ambiguity and irony, readers of the short story can come to disparate evaluations of Grant's behaviour. Both extremes, to condemn Grant for deceiving Fiona or to approve of Grant's altruism for the benefit of Fiona's wellbeing, are too simple assessments of a complex situation. Instead, Munro's narrative induces the reader to reflect on "a moral philosophy which rises above conformity" as Ventura explains with regard to Munro's omission of any explicit explanation of the true nature of Grant's behaviour:

Munro leaves unuttered the terms of Aubrey's return. This powerful ellipsis [...] highlights her commitment to a moral philosophy which rises above conformity to the moral values of the community and commits itself to more complex and more covert ethical principles, of which silence, restraint and reticence are significant components. (par. 30)

Conclusion

Alice Munro's short story illustrates the challenges which age-related diseases, such as dementia and Alzheimer's disease, entail for the individual. It suggests the importance of traces of the past in the context of memory and memory loss. Whereas traces help to remember the past life and the personality of a patient suffering from dementia, they also confront the patients and their relatives with what is lost due to dementia since "it is always a passage that it [the trace] indicates, not some possible presence" (Ricoeur 124). As a result, considerations of traces may comfort the patient and relative but they can also complicate a person's coming to terms with the disease and cause emotional distress as presented in Munro's fictional character Grant.

Against the background of the severe impact of dementia on the patients' and their relatives' lives, Munro's story engages the reader in reflections on traditional conceptions of ethics and moral behaviour. In the process of reading and recapitulating the plot and the characters presented in "The Bear Came Over the Mountain" the reader is able to continuously reshape a narrative identity. The reader can apply his or her experiences gained through immersion in the story world – as well as through the effects which narrative empathy, identification with, or emotional distance from the fictional characters have on him or her – to the real world. Munro's story induces the reader to contemplate the models for action presented in the narrative as well as on the reader's own moral behaviour. The severe effects dementia has on the patients themselves, their relatives, and caretakers and the unremitting advance of the disease may demand ethical principles that deviate from the established norms of a community. As a result of the contrast between Grant's selfless behaviour and his return to traces of his old egotistical self, Munro's narrative offers the reader ambiguous proposals for ethical reflection, just as requested by Ricoeur who concludes: "Still it belongs to the reader, now an agent, an initiator of action, to choose among the multiple proposals of ethical justice brought forth by reading." (249)

REFERENCES

Assmann, Aleida. *Cultural Memory and Western Civilization: Functions, Media, Archives*. New York: Cambridge UP, 2011. Print.

Assmann, Jan. *Cultural Memory and Early Civilization: Writing, Remembrance, and Political Imagination*. New York: Cambridge UP, 2011. Print.

"Best Sellers." *New York Times* 4 May 2014. Web. 29 April 2014.

Couser, G. Thomas. *Memoir: An Introduction*. Oxford: Oxford UP, 2012. Print.

Davis, Boyd, and Margaret Maclagan. "Talking with Maureen: Extenders and Formulaic Language in Small Stories and Canonical Narratives." *Dialogue and Dementia – Cognitive and Communicative Resources for Engagement*. Ed. Robert W. Schrauf and Nicole Müller. New York: Psychology P, 2014. 87-120. Print.

Franzen, Jonathan. "'Runaway': Alice's Wonderland." *New York Times* 14 Nov. 2004. Web. 8 July 2014.

Hoffman, Martin L. "Empathy, Social Cognition, and Moral Action." *Handbook of Moral Behavior and Development. Vol. 1: Theory.* Ed. William M. Kurtines and Jacob L. Gerwirtz. New York: Psychology P, 2014. 275-302. Print.

Hooper, Brad. *The Fiction of Alice Munro: An Appreciation.* Westport: Praeger, 2008. Print.

Keen, Suzanne. "Narrative Empathy." *The Living Handbook of Narratology.* Ed. Peter Hühn, et al. Hamburg: Hamburg U. Web. 24 Nov. 2014.

Littré, Emile. *Dictionnaire de la langue française* 7 vols. Paris: Hachette, 1965. Print.

McGill, Robert. "No Nation but Adaptation: 'The Bear Came over the Mountain,' Away from Her and What It Means to be Faithful." *Canadian Literature/Littérature Canadienne: A Quarterly of Criticism and Review* 197 (Summer 2008): 98-111. Print.

Munro, Alice. "The Bear Came Over the Mountain." *New Yorker* 27 Dec. 1999 and 21 Oct. 2013. Web. 25 July 2014.

---. "The Bear Came Over the Mountain." *Hateship, Friendship, Courtship, Loveship, Marriage.* London: Chatto & Windus, 2001. 275-323. Print.

Ricoeur, Paul. *Time and Narrative.* Vol. 3. Trans. Kathleen Blamey and David Pellauer. Chicago: U of Chicago P, 2008. Print.

Venema, Henry. "Paul Ricoeur on Refigurative Reading and Narrative Identity." *Symposium* 4:2 (Autumn 2000): 237-48.

Ventura, Héliane. "The Skald and the Goddess: Reading 'The Bear Came Over the Mountain' by Alice Munro." The Short Stories of Alice Munro. Spec. issue of *Journal of the Short Story in English* 55 (Autumn 2010): 2-10. Web. 3 July 2015. <http://jsse.revues.org/1121?lang=fr.>

Yagoda, Ben. *Memoir: A History.* New York: Riverhead, 2009. Print.

Horror Mortis, Structural Trauma, and Postmodern Parody in Saul Bellow's *Henderson the Rain King*

FRANCISCO COLLADO-RODRÍGUEZ

THE NOVELIST'S GAME WITH FRAMEWORKS

Criticism, Freudian psychoanalysis, and myth symbolism

This paper begins by laying out its critical objectives, evaluating existing criticism on Bellow's novel *Henderson the Rain King* (1959), and adding a narratological analysis that may reveal the ideological significance of one of the writer's most remarkable aims in his work: the parody of two critical frameworks that had become rather popular in the post-war period, even if they had originated in modernist times. Symbols and conceits taken from Freudian psychoanalysis – eventually revitalised in contemporary Trauma Studies – and myth criticism, as well as their persistent symbol-hunting methodology, result in what seems to be a comical and entertaining novel that, however, hides a profound criticism of WASP ideology and its manifestation in 20th-century American colonialism. In his essay "A Jewish Writer in America," published soon before his death, Bellow measured the condition of being an American writer of Jewish origin and elaborated on his belief that the "dislike of Jews was a ready way for WASP literati to identify themselves with the great [American] tradition," giving names of famous poets and intellectuals of the early 20th century and explicitly citing Henry Adams' anti-Dreyfusard position (3). Protagonist Eugene Henderson, a psychologically castrated and castrating individual who is also structurally traumatised by the notion of death, offers in his own self-descriptions a *condensation* (remember Freud's interpretation of dreams) of the most contemptible traits frequently attributed to the American right-wing of Anglo-Saxon Puritan descent. Additionally, Henderson tries to *displace* (Freud again) his problems to the alleged primitive cradle of civilization, Africa, where he undergoes some of the most well-known stages of the hero's quest.

The following pages aim to show that Bellow's basic strategies to carry out both his parody of the two modernist frameworks of myth and psychoanalysis and his ideological attack are his use of a narrator whose words cannot be trusted and his deployment of an excessive use of symbols and motifs. In so doing, the essay's final aim is to inscribe *Henderson the Rain King* as a postmodern novel due to its overloaded staging of humans as symbol-making creatures, trapped in the world as text but also to link this relocation to Henderson's portrait as a structurally traumatised and pathetic WASP "hero" who tries to find in Africa the existential and sociological answers that may quench his desire to know what *he wants*. This paper also challenges the frequent critical assumptions that identify Bellow's protagonist as a neo-humanist hero who represents his author's concern with Freudian, transcendentalist, or existentialist interpretations of life and who is finally able to attain wisdom and improve his character and mental stability.

Narratology is used as a critical method of enquiry. This well-known textual method for narrative analysis is based on the scrutiny of the two ontological levels existing in any narrative text: the story and the discourse or narrating process. The method also draws upon the importance of different elements in the construction of the narrative world: the voice or narrator (evaluating its different types), the focalization or point of view (also recognizable in various forms), and the use of space and temporality (Genette). The following diagram summarises the most important levels and notions that our analysis needs to address in *Henderson the Rain King* to uncover the writer's ideological and parodic aims:

External level: Bellow and readers

Implied author (ironic or parodic implications of the text)

Discourse or narrating level: Henderson as narrator

Story level: Events and characters
Henderson as protagonist

Implied or ideal reader (capable of tracing the authorial use of irony and parody)

Having put forth the aims and methodology of this paper, it would seem necessary to establish the research territory by revising significant studies on Bellow's novel that, even after realizing – in some cases – the writer's parodic approach, have interpreted the novel as a (modernist) Bildungsroman or as the narrative of a successful (comic) quest for existential meaning. Some examples and quotations to demonstrate the persistent popularity of this traditional understanding of the novel should be cited to validate our approach and its addition to existing criticism of the novel. Daniel Fuchs' classic interpretation of Bellow's novel remarked on the writer's (modernist) mythic mood while also acknowledging the importance of parody in the novel: "Myth serves the cause of personal transcendence; the primitive, the voice of civilization; the heart of darkness, the heart of light. As some of the critics have noticed, [Henderson] is a parody of Conrad, Lawrence, Hemingway, rather than another note on the decline of the West" (79). However, Fuchs' significant study still evaluated the novel as Bellow's attempt to create a new comedy where the protagonist's hypochondriac condition is only a source of humour (81-82). More recent criticism though has been concerned with other issues that analyse Henderson's role from multiple perspectives, but the narrator's unreliable condition and the textual and ideological trap set for the readers by the excessive parody and symbolism have not been given sufficient attention in any of them. A few years ago, Dan Muhlestein quantified the most relevant aims of criticism the novel has received since its publication in 1959:

> The philosophical underpinnings of Henderson have been discussed almost ad nauseam, including whether – and to what extent – the novel either embodies or critiques existentialism, transcendentalism, Jamesian psychology, Reichian ideas, alienation theory, and science. Literary sources and influences have also been traced, including debts to such diverse authors as Blake, Browning, Cervantes, Eliot, Wordsworth, and the authors of the Bible. The most consequential intertextual analysis has focused on Bellow's use of anthropological source material – especially the work of Burton and Herskovits – and on his anxiety-of-influence reaction against Conrad, Hemingway, and the modern novel generally. (59)

This paper questions previous critical understandings of Bellow's novel as a modernist piece and denies that its author developed a neo-humanist critique. It elaborates on Fuchs' (and others') perception of the book's parody by arguing that Bellow's hyper-parodic tools are a strategy to criticise and condense white patriarchal self-righteousness, cold fascist modernist intellectualism, and American colonialism in the figure of Henderson. These authorial critical tools systematically present death as the enervating drive that forces the protagonist into pathetic and anti-heroic deeds.

Even in recent years, some critics are still haunted by Henderson's "success" as a mythic hero. Along the conventional line of criticism mentioned above, Rhea Thomas concludes in her study on the metaphysics of fear in the novel that "during his African quest, [Henderson] discovers a new purpose for life. The power of love, fear's opposite, awakens his soul to the beauty present in the world, even if the world contains suffering. The reality of love, past or present, transcends all fear" (45).[1] However, in 1979 Clayton was already quoting Bellow's ironic words on *Henderson* which many critics have apparently disregarded ever since: "'You want a symbolic novel?' the novelist asked, 'I'll give you the most symbolic novel you ever wrote a critical article about'" (169-70).

---

1   On this see also Schechner 220-26; 31; and Zarate 41.

HENDERSON AS HYPER-TRAUMATISED HERO AND HENDERSON THE RAIN KING AS PARODIC NOVEL

In the first chapters of the novel, following in the best bourgeois conventions of the genre, the protagonist offers a comic description of his previous life and social status. When filtered through a narratological analysis, Henderson's account and self-description already shows that, despite earlier and current criticism, Bellow writes his book framed in a postmodern perspective which is saturated by *too many* modernist concerns about the meaning of life, its brevity, and the necessity of mythic transcendence, a condition of excessive symbolism that already discloses the importance that cultural parody will acquire in the novel. By parodying two recurrent frameworks of the first decades of the 20th century, psychoanalytic Freudianism and the Eliotian "mythic method," Bellow's ironic approach to modernist existential worries stresses human incapacity to comprehend reality in fully objective terms. Henderson is a grotesque mentally-wrecked person and all his digressions about death and mortality only reveal that he is parodically trapped in circularity; he may become aware of cultural traces and long for an alleged better past, as the high-modernists did, but he can never retrieve the (myth of the) origins of his personal want. In other words, the novelist *methodically* builds his postmodern frame by resorting to an excessive number of symbols and situations that typify both an exaggerated (post- and) Freudian understanding of being as structurally traumatised and a modernist (naïve and proto-fascist) interpretation of the individual as a mythic hero on a quest in search of a never-attainable illumination that might dispel the ghosts of human mortality.

By the time the novel was published, some writers were already carrying out a sustained use of parody as a literary correlate of the pervasive (and poststructuralist) notion that the human being is trapped in a semiotic web, the world as text, from which it is impossible to escape. Often, relevant theorists of postmodernism, such as Patricia Waugh (*Metafiction*), Linda Hutcheon (*A Poetics of Postmodernism*), or Edmund Smyth (*Postmodernism and Contemporary Fiction*), stressed this meaning to explain that experimental strategies are mainly the result of metafictional and parodic practices which describe life as the prison-house of language. The issue led Canadian critic Linda Hutcheon to formulate her well-known definition of (postmodern) parody as "repetition that includes difference [...] it is imitation with critical ironic distance, whose irony can cut both ways. Ironic versions of 'trans-contextualization' and inversion are its major formal operatives, and the range of pragmatic ethos is from scornful ridicule to reverential homage" (*A Theory of Parody* 37). As the following pages will show, Bellow's use of parody in *Henderson the Rain King* is much closer to scornful ridicule than to any reverential homage dedicated to rich American whites.

The narratological analysis discloses, from the first page of the book, Bellow's ironic approach to his narrator's report by overtly questioning the latter's reliability as a reporter of truthful events. The postmodern cultural relativist assumption that narrative can never represent reality in truthful or objective terms is re-enforced from the beginning of the story. The narrative strategies that the writer deployed to construct his book helped him to turn it into a sustained parody of Freudianism and myth criticism, but the type of narrator-protagonist he chose for his novel insistently points at his purpose of denouncing the American WASP ideological colonialism of the world. Our narratological evaluation starts, then, by considering that Henderson is a figure that functions both as narrator and as protagonist of the story. This fact reveals at the very beginning of the book, *pace* many of Bellow's critics, that his alleged quest for existential renewal has failed. Being a narrator in retrospect, the events in the story he tells are already finished at the time when he starts to narrate them, but he still offers clear indications of his traumatised condition which decidedly show that his modernist quest for meaning and mental health has been unsuccessful:

What made me take this trip to Africa? There is no quick explanation. Things got worse and worse and worse and pretty soon they were too complicated.
When *I think* of my condition at the age of fifty-five when I bought the ticket, *all is grief*. The facts begin to crowd me and soon *I get a pressure* in the chest. A disorderly rush *begins* – my parents, my wives, my girls, my children, my farm, my animals, my habits, my money, my music lessons, my drunkenness, my prejudices, my brutality, my teeth, my face, my soul! *I have* to cry, "No, no, get back, curse you, let me alone!" But how can they let me alone? *They belong* to me. *They are* mine. And *they pile* into me from all sides. It turns into chaos.
However, the world which I thought so mighty an oppressor has removed its wrath from me. But *if I am to make sense* to you people and explain why I went to Africa I

must face up to the fact. I might as well start with the money. I am rich. From my old man I inherited three million dollars after taxes, but I thought myself a bum and had my reasons, the main reason being that I behaved like a bum. But privately when things got very bad I often looked into books to see whether I could find some helpful words, and one day I read, "The forgiveness of things is perpetual and righteousness first is not required." This impressed me so deeply that I went around saying it to myself. But then I forgot which book it was. It was one of thousands left by my father, who had also written a number of them. (3; emphasis added)

We should first notice the contrastive deployment of different tenses. Henderson frequently uses the present to refer to his condition at the moment he is narrating (see the added emphasis) and the past to refer to the anxious situations that led him to take the trip to Africa, in an attempt to find existential regeneration. The present tense revels that at the time he decides to narrate his adventure – once his African experience is over – Henderson is still a highly neurotic person who shows clear symptoms of paranoia. Remembering his condition when he bought his ticket to Africa, all is still "grief" and he again suffers from the disorderly rush exemplified by an accumulation of factors that eventually cause a somatic reaction manifested as a pressure in his chest. His life – in his narrating present – "turns into chaos." Despite this, he is not ready to admit that his mental troubles have not disappeared: "the world which I thought so mighty an oppressor has removed its wrath from me." Has it? Has his African quest brought about a (modernist) epiphany to end his troubles? Clearly, it has not. Henderson – as many other narrator-protagonists – is totally unreliable.

The next pages in the book offer Henderson's report about his infancy, as well as his manners, economic situation, and some specific events. As narrator, Henderson thinks that those events and manners – especially his rage, which could have caused the death of Miss Lenox, Henderson's frail old maid – motivated his decision to go to Africa in search of an existential solution for his anxiety. The sense of increasing problems in Henderson's life is one of the main cards played by Bellow to describe his personage's hyper-problematic condition, parody Freudianism, and criticise WASP ideology. Readers interested in psychology may conclude that Henderson is a perfect example of a Freudian castrated man who, in his self-confessing report, epitomises many situations described in *The Interpretation of Dreams*. In the excerpt above, Henderson illustrates the existence of a demanding castrating father, an intellectual – friend to William James and anti-Dreyfusard Henry Adams – who wrote several books, played the violin, and always favoured Henderson's brother, ironically named Dick.

"My father," the narrator confesses, "was a big man, solid and clean" (13). He also had a particular use for money. The symbolic fatherly link between finances and culture is rather explicit in his case: "I search through dozens of volumes, but all that turned up was money, for my father had used currency for bookmarks" (3). In reaction to his super-ego's demands, Henderson decides to breed pigs on the property that he inherited from his exclusive WASP family, where his great-grandfather had been Secretary of State and his great-uncles had been ambassadors to England and France (7). The result of his present condition, as he himself realises, is modernist decadence – "December ruins of my frozen state" (33). In addition, as mentioned above, Henderson has money in excess. Accordingly, he also is of a disproportionate weight and size. Even his sentimental life needs to be excessive. He describes his divorce from his first wife following his cheating on her, the intricacies of his second marriage, and the fact that he also mistreats his second wife, that he has had several mistresses, and that women suffocate him (4-7). He refuses to acknowledge that his 15-year-old daughter has given birth to a mixed-race baby (32-37). To add to the long list of circumstances in the narrator's life that would "prove" his extremely neurotic condition and his masochistic need for punishment, Bellow incorporates another symbolic event that befalls Henderson when he is already in Africa. He breaks an artificial dental bridge ("My whole body was trembling when I spat out those molars, and I thought, 'Maybe you've lived too long, Henderson,'" [129]). The episode soon drew the attention of early critics of the novel who understood it as a metaphor for the fact that decadent Henderson had broken his bridge with reality but also as symbolic proof that he was a castrated man: loss of teeth being such a symbol for loss of virility in *The Interpretation of Dreams* (244-45).

Along the first pages in the novel, the authorial irony used on Henderson's figure can be recognised not only in the protagonist's excessive number of traumatizing episodes but also in his inability to distinguish his own humour as racist and the fact that he is continuously mistreating people. Henderson is a white Anglo-Saxon millionaire who makes the decision to breed pigs in his property while talking to a Jewish friend (20) but he is also ready to make a joke about the exclusion of

Jewish-Americans from vacation resorts (7). Other events and manners reflected in his self-portrait progressively mark him as a more and more pathetic, even if at times comical, idiot, and an ill-tempered rich man. So, when he goes to Africa looking for an answer to his existential anguish, he does so as the chaperone of a recently married couple who have decided to go to Africa for their honeymoon. He needs to keep his head covered at all times, and his behaviour is frequently violent and aggressive – he has a pistol range in his mansion and joined the Army to fight in WW2 even though he was already too old for the service In other words, Henderson becomes a condensation of the most hideous and aggressive traits frequently attributed to American WASPs and, more specifically, to the builders of American political supremacy in the 20th century (from lion-hunter President Roosevelt to post-war Presidents Truman and Eisenhower): he is wealthy but inconsiderate, behaves like a derelict even if he owns an ample library, embraces violence, weapons, and militarism, mistreats women and non-whites, and fails as father, husband, and friend. He is anything but a hero figure. And Bellow's astute revenge on the American WASP centres on the understandable existence of an internal voice in Henderson's repressed self, which he frequently hears: *I want, I want!* What might a WASP want?

HENDERSON'S STRUCTURALLY TRAUMATISED SELF

Horror mortis, animal symbolism, and the call to Henderson's monomythic adventure

The first pages of the novel also introduce three motifs whose obsessive repetition and self-conscious nature point to the undefeated state of Henderson's horror mortis condition. He confesses over and over again that he hears a voice whose meaning he cannot interpret, he compares himself to different animals on several occasions, and he blames himself for the death of Miss Lenox, reporting on the event at different times during the narrative.

The first time he reports on the existence of his inner voice he is climbing up a staircase to have sex with Lily, his would-be second wife: "a ceaseless voice in my heart that said, *I want, I want, I want, oh, I want –*

yes, go on, I said to myself, *Strike, strike, strike, strike!*" (12). Although the passage seems to associate Henderson's needs to his sexuality, it also anticipates (*strike*) that in his African adventure his *want* will always lead him to do something violent: in classic Freudian terms, his want will progressively turn from libidinous to thanatic. The insistent repetition of his inner voice throughout the pages of the book clearly points to an unsatisfying desire and as soon as the protagonist establishes contact with the first native tribe in Africa, Queen Willatale will associate its meaning with existentialist despair, an interpretation that Henderson understands as an epiphany but that will relieve his anxiety only momentarily.

The narrator's second obsession consists of comparing himself to different animals, a repetitive trope also leading to existentialist issues, finally crystallizing in Henderson's perception of King Dahfu's theories about animals as another transcendental or ultimate answer to his plight. On a trip to France with Lily, which precedes his journey to Africa, the protagonist visits an aquarium where he experiences a negative (modernist) epiphany at a moment of the day, the twilight, which brings direct echoes from the stoppage of the mythic circle in Eliot's *The Waste Land*:

They keep a marine station there, and I had a strange experience in the aquarium. It was twilight. I looked in at an octopus, and the creature seemed also to look at me and press its soft head to the glass, flat, the flesh becoming pale and granular—blanched, speckled. The eyes spoke to me coldly. But even more speaking, even more cold, was the soft head with its speckles, and the Brownian motion of those speckles, a cosmic coldness in which I felt I was dying [....] "This is my last day. Death is giving me notice." (19)

The passage has been quoted frequently by critics who focus on Henderson's condition as an existentialist trap for its apparent symbolism but, within the spectrum of the different interpretations the scene may offer, I wish to draw attention to two aspects that strengthen the perspectives provided in this paper: 1) Henderson *as narrator* uses a synaesthesia – "The eyes spoke to me coldly" – that combines three different senses or attributes into the same feeling, thereby stressing the impact of an experience that still persists in the narrator's present, a horror mortis or negative revelation that has not abandoned him since; 2) The animal chosen for this bleak epiphany is described as a huge head with big eyes and eight tentacles with which it takes food to its beak. The octopus is supposed to be the most intelligent of the invertebrates and in his act of reflection Henderson becomes attracted to its pale skin which presents however many speckles, or dirty spots. Brains, killing power, white skin, dirt, the octopus and its many tentacles may also be understood as a condensed metaphor of American WASP colonialism and of Henderson looking at his own reflection in a mirror. Together with his inner "*I want*," the octopus experience will come back to the narrator on several occasions during his telling of his African adventure on which his final aim, as recommended by Dahfu, will be to become a lion even if he is still aware as narrator that he can never be more than a bear.

The third event that he also repeats obsessively is Miss Lenox's death. This character appears to play a minor role in the story; she comes daily to Henderson's mansion to fix his breakfast—"this was my only need at the time" (26). One winter morning, when he has been yelling at the table, he finds her dead in the kitchen, an added existential experience that terrifies Henderson both in his past as protagonist of the story and again in his present as narrator of it:

During my rage her heart had stopped [...] I turned off the gas. Dead! Her small, toothless face, to which I laid my knuckles, was growing cold. The soul, like a current of air, like a draft, like a bubble, sucked out of the window. I stared at her. So, this is it, the end – farewell? And all this while, these days and weeks, the wintry garden had been speaking to me of this fact and no other; and till this moment I had not understood what this gray and white and brown, the bark, the snow, the twigs, had been telling me. (39)

The narrator's ambiguous metaphysical position in the passage above should be pointed out. At this new horror mortis experience, he is ready to mix the Christian belief in the soul with the more primitive belief, brought back by modernist intellectuals, in the mythic cycles of nature as mirrors of human life. Once Nietzsche had proclaimed the death of God in the modern world in *Twilight of the Idols* (45), modernist artists turned again to more primitive interpretations of life for existential support and many found in the field of anthropology and comparative religion, epitomised in James Frazer's *The Golden Bough*, relevant scholarly sources to justify the return to a mythic understanding of reality (Manganaro 1-67). Miss Lenox's death produces in Henderson a metaphysical shiver, inducing him to abandon his former life on his family property and go to Africa in search of existential replenishment. He talks to himself in a new process of self-reflection, again showing apparent ambiguous beliefs about religion and mortality: "So for God's sake make a move, Henderson, put forth effort. You too will die of pestilence. Death will annihilate you and nothing will remain, and there will be nothing left but junk [...]. For the sake of all, get out" (40). Despite invoking the name of God in vain, his existentialist fear when contemplating Miss Lenox's cadaver produces in him what qualifies as a mythic but parodic "Call to Adventure" (Campbell 45-54). His decision to take arms against the sea of his WASP existential troubles contrasts with the many times he has threatened his wife Lily with committing suicide or his confession that he is also troubled by melancholia (*Henderson* 14). Obviously, readers may also see in his choice a parody of Camus' Sisyphus who decides to face the odds and discard suicide as an escape from a universe where man is out of harmony. Within the more recent critical field of Trauma Studies, it is interesting to mention that in Dominick LaCapra's views structural trauma results from the subject's realization of the intrinsic mortality of the human condition. This scholar associates trauma with the existentialist plight, a condition that displays itself in frequent states of anxiety and melancholia as well as in other symptoms including uncontrollable repetitions or ticks, or states of panic, which also fit in Henderson's self-portrait (76-85). Following Camus' existentialist thinking and LaCapra's considerations above, we might conclude that the traumatic fate of the individual becomes tragic when he becomes conscious of his mortality. However, once he has become conscious of his mortality, Henderson's fate becomes more a parody than a tragedy.

THE HERO'S QUEST OR THE ANTI-HEROIC AMERICAN WASP

Once in Africa, Henderson experiences a number of adventures that critics have frequently linked to *Heart of Darkness* or Ernest Hemingway's stories about the African continent. Certainly, parodic connections between Eugene Henderson and the narrator of Conrad's novel or sharing the same initials with the author of *The Snows of Kilimanjaro* are topics too obvious to be ignored but there is another issue much more interesting for the purpose of this paper: Bellow's excessively traumatised protagonist also fulfils a Jungian quest to get rid of his personality troubles, a quest that coincides for all intents and purposes with Joseph Campbell's pattern in *The Hero With a Thousand Faces*.[2] Once again, a typical modernist framework – myth narrative – is followed in an excessively detailed way. We should not forget that in 1937 Saul Bellow had already graduated with honours in anthropology and sociology which means that he was acquainted with modernist anthropology and Jung's archetypical or mythic process of individuation laid out in "The Archetypes of the Collective Unconscious." Ten years before the publication of *Henderson the Rain King*, the American anthropologist Joseph Campbell had published the first edition of his influential book where he developed a cultural model that he named *the Hero's quest* or monomyth, the pattern that Bellow follows almost to the letter in *Henderson the Rain King*.

Campbell asserts in the first pages of his book that his anthropological approach relies heavily on Freud's and Jung's frameworks and relevant symbolism to interpret human behaviour (4-13). The anthropologist works from premises that qualify him as a believer in the modernist master narrative of myth (Manganaro 151-85). He develops the pattern of the monomyth in an attempt to demonstrate that many rituals, legends and stories in many different cultures and times reflect the Jungian idea that the ultimate meaning of life can be found in one's inner self, a notion that critics have systematically associated with the modernist motif of the "inner gaze." The monomyth represents both the physical journey of the hero in different cultural manifestations and the psychic journey of the individual on a quest for the meaning of his or her own life.

Campbell divides the hero's pattern into three main stages (departure, initiation, and return) which he splits into minor motifs, symbols or situations. He asserts that the monomyth motifs cannot be "identical in the various parts of the globe" (389). However, in the case of *Henderson the Rain King* the narrator describes his African adventure in terms that fit perfectly into every one of Campbell's motifs. Henderson is "called into adventure" (first motif) when, as already mentioned, he *interprets* that one of his fits of anger has killed Miss Lenox. Then, he mentally condemns his anger and addresses himself, "So for God's sake make a move, Henderson,

---

2 See Rodrigues.

put forth effort" (*Henderson* 40), and decides to accompany his friend Charlie and his wife on their honeymoon to Africa, "the ancient bed of mankind" (42). The event signals the early association of his quest to the idea of death and existential panic.

However, once in Africa Henderson becomes a hilarious parody of the white explorer, always wearing his helmet where he hides the ultimate protection humans have in contemporary society: money, a few thousand-dollar bills that will play "magic" and finally get him out of trouble when he decides to flee Africa. He soon has an argument with Charlie and continues on his own adventure with the sole company of a black employee, Romilayu. The assistant's wisdom and experience qualifies here as the first "(Supernatural) Aid," another Campbellian situation. Then Henderson needs to "cross the first threshold" that will take him into what Campbell denominates "the land of magnifying power" where the Jungian quest for the meaning of life is going to unfold. The first threshold – representing a dive into the waters of the unconscious – is symbolically crossed when, led by Romilayu, Henderson walks across the Arnewi river, a pathetic version of the Stygian lake because, due to a long-lasting drought, the river is dry (47).

Once the hero is on the other side of the threshold, the process of initiation starts which frequently means that the protagonist has to begin his "Road of Trials" by defeating the guardian of the threshold – the Can Cerberus that represents the first manifestation of the Jungian shadow (Campbell 77-98). In Henderson's case, the crossing of the first threshold manifests itself in his confrontation with Prince Itelo: "Your Highness," Henderson tells him, "I am kind of on a quest" (*Henderson* 65). Itelo is a cultivated Prince of the naïve Arnewi tribe. He can speak English and has attended a mission school in Syria in the company of Dahfu, the present king of the violent Wariri tribe, whom Henderson will visit after his experiences among the Arnewi. Tradition holds that newcomers fight in a ritual battle with Itelo and so Henderson does, being crowned the winner (63-70). The Arnewi Prince also tells him what his people's main problem is: Their water reservoir is infected with frogs and the tribe thinks that it is a curse. Then Henderson is introduced to Willatale, Queen of the Arnewi and Itelo's aunt, and to her sister Mtalba. Both are big women "of substance" but whereas the Queen represents the motif of the "Meeting with the Goddess" or Jungian encounter with the archetype of the anima, her sister is an archetypical "Temptress" who tries to lure Henderson into a sexual bond (Campbell 109-126). In Jungian terms, the part of our personality symbolised by the anima archetype may be both positive and negative, goddess and temptress, but in the novel, both sides show themselves to Henderson at the same time, in one more example of parodic excess. From the Queen Henderson will receive what he thinks is an existential epiphany: His anxious interior voice that repeats *I want, I want* is translated by Willatale as *Grun-tu-molani*, literarily "man wants to live." However, Henderson receives the epiphany while noticing at the same time that Mtalba "was looking into my eyes meltingly" (85).

Self-confident that his is the role of the white explorer who has come to help the poor natives, Henderson decides to get rid of the reservoir frogs by killing them with a homemade bomb. In effect, he kills the frogs but the explosion also breaks the dam and releases the water, which the dry soil immediately drains (109-10). His paternalist behaviour and pathetic self-assurance once again brings about the misery of others. Still believing in his role as hero, Henderson leaves the Arnewi in shame to cross a second threshold that, this time, is activated by a different Campbellian situation: the "Belly of the Whale," a symbol of the hero's passage into the land of magnifying power metaphorised by Jonah's biblical story (90-94). Henderson and Romilayu are captured by the Wariri and put into a dark hut where the WASP millionaire, while eating a hard biscuit, breaks some of his teeth and his bridge. As with Jonah, this becomes a long dark night of expiation for him (*Henderson* 120). The parodic hero is ready to "resurrect" once again and finally encounter the last of the Jungian archetypes that should bring him to the final revelation about his life and his anxious reactions to it. The motif of the "Atonement with the Father," a Campbellian symbol for the assimilation of the Jungian archetype of meaning (or the Wise Man), is fulfilled by Henderson when Dahfu, King of the Wariri, decides to mentor him. From Dahfu he will learn about the supreme male power represented by the lion and will experience his Campbellian "Apotheosis" when he becomes, in one more ritualistic act, the Rain King of the tribe. He raises the heavy image of Mummah, the earth mother, an event that as narrator he remembers as another moment of revelation: "My spirit was awake and it welcomed life anew. Damn the whole thing! Life anew! I was still alive and kicking and I had the old grun-tu-molani" (193).

Ironically, Dahfu's teachings depict not only the peculiar situation of a young black man giving advice to a bigger older white American man dressed as an explorer, they also add to many other symbolic references to animal life present in the novel. Henderson breeds pigs but he thinks of himself as a bear, he trembles at the sight of an octopus but then follows Dahfu's instructions to meet a lioness. When Dahfu is killed by a lion, he is fulfilling a rite that is perfectly adapted to the fertility rituals described by Frazer in *The Golden Bough*. He is the King who represents the land and as such his strength is reflected in that land and when he dies, Henderson as Rain King has to replace him and occupy the throne. However, the hero prefers to escape, the main reason for his flight being that as new king of the tribe he has to fertilise the land symbolically. In practice, it means that the American "explorer" needs to give satisfaction to over thirty wives and concubines, which does not seem to be the best job for his apparently castrated self ("And anyway, I am no stud," 315).

In such a ritual-filled narrative, the hero's escape from the Wariri fits into even more Campbellian situations. He has to escape by fighting against another guardian of the threshold, this time an amazon (324). However, he takes his prize with him, the lion cub that symbolises Dahfu's royal spirit, and together with Romilayu they start a (Campbellian magic) "flight" (326). When already in a safe village, Henderson becomes the "Master of the Two Worlds" by experiencing several weeks of dreams and hallucinations that keep him hovering between consciousness and unconscious (328-329). When he finally takes an actual flight back to America, his plane lands in the symbolic Newfoundland for refuelling and, with the help of the lion cub, he establishes a friendship with a little Persian boy whose words he cannot understand: but who needs words after having experienced all those revelations?

Campbell's last motif, "Freedom to Live" (238-243), represents the final epiphanic moment in which the hero allegedly becomes conscious of the meaning of life. Henderson, in his role as narrator, cannot refer more explicitly to his *freedom* at that moment in Newfoundland, and he ends his narrative in an apparent state of happiness that, however, is charged with authorial irony: "The great, beautiful propellers were still, all four of them. I guess I felt it was my turn now to move, and so went running—leaping, leaping, pounding, and tingling over the pure white lining of the fray Arctic silence" (*Henderson* 341). The realization of pure white in the cold North appears to make him happy, but the landscape, which ends in silence, in its whiteness and cold resembles Henderson's description of his existential state of panic while contemplating the octopus' "cosmic coldness" (19). Furthermore, the implications that the narratological analysis uncover in Henderson's narrative clearly indicate that even if his remembrance of the Newfoundland episode makes the narrator temporarily happy, Henderson's mental condition does not qualify as the one of the hero who has understood the meaning of life. By playing with the post-war critics' methodological propensity for looking for Freudian and myth symbols, Bellow elaborated a sustained parody of modernist frameworks and, at the same time, he linked white Anglo-Saxon intellectuals and their proto-fascist high-brow ideology to the cold stare associated with the realization of death.

This essay has aimed to analyse Bellow's parodic postmodern approach in his novel *Henderson the Rain King*, with specific examples corresponding to each of the two frames targeted by the novelist: Henderson's excessive (Freudian) neurotic condition as both protagonist and narrator and his too perfectly detailed fulfilment of the monomyth pattern. In cases such as *Henderson the Rain King,* textual strategies that respond to the author's criticism of different but complementary frameworks may lead scholars, as I think is true here, to conclude that they are symptoms of the artist's cultural shift from the modernist to the postmodernist ethos but also that there is an underpinning, more covert purpose in the author's conscious manipulation of the traces of a past cultural period: to force his readers to ideological reflections on a present still suffocated by the cold colonialist stare of the white oppressors.

REFERENCES

Bellow, Saul. "A Jewish Writer in America." *New York Review of Books*, 27 Oct. 2011. Print.
---. *Henderson the Rain King*. Harmondsworth: Penguin, 1976. Print.
Campbell, Joseph. *The Hero With a Thousand Faces*. Princeton: Princeton UP, 1968. Print.
Camus, Albert. *The Myth of Sisyphus*. Trans. Justin O'Brien. London: Penguin, 1988. Print.

Clayton, John Jacob. *Saul Bellow: In Defense of Man*. Bloomington: Indiana UP, 1979. Print.

Cronin, Gloria L. *A Room of His Own: In Search of the Feminine in the Novels of Saul Bellow*. Syracuse: Syracuse UP, 2001. Print.

Eliot, T.S. *The Waste Land, Prufrock and Other Poems*. Mineola: Dover P, 1998.

Frazer, James George. *The Golden Bough: A Study in Magic and Religion*. Oxford: Oxford UP, 1994. Print.

Freud, Sigmund. *The Interpretation of Dreams*. Trans. A. A. Brill. London: Allen & Unwin, 1932. Print.

Fuchs, Daniel. *Saul Bellow: Vision and Revision*. Durham: Duke UP, 1984. Print.

Genette, Gerard. *Narrative Discourse*. Ithaca: Cornell UP, 1980. Print.

Hutcheon, Linda. *A Poetics of Postmodernism: History, Theory, Fiction*. New York: Routledge, 1988. Print.

---. *A Theory of Parody: The Teachings of Twentieth-Century Art Forms*. London: Methuen, 1985. Print.

Jung, Carl G. "The Archetypes of the Collective Unconscious." *The Collected Works, vol. 9, Part I*. Ed. Herbert Read, et al. London: Routledge and Kegan Paul, 1971. Print.

LaCapra, Dominick. *Writing History, Writing Trauma*. Baltimore: Johns Hopkins UP, 2001. Print.

Lyotard, Jean-François. *The Postmodern Condition: A Report on Knowledge*. Manchester: Manchester UP, 1984. Print.

Manganaro, Marc. *Myth, Rhetoric, and the Voice of Authority: A Critique of Frazer, Eliot, Frye, and Campbell*. New Haven: Yale UP, 1992. Print.

Muhlestein, Dan. "Wrestling With Angels: Male Friendship in *Henderson the Rain King*." *Saul Bellow Journal* 21.1-2 (2005): 41-61. Print.

Nietzsche, Friedrich. *Twilight of the Idols*. Trans. Duncan Large. Oxford: Oxford UP, 1998. Print.

Rodrigues, Eusebio L. "Saul Bellow's Henderson as Mankind and Messiah." *Renascence* 35.4 (Summer 1983): 235-46. Print.

Schechner, Mark. "Jewish Fiction." *Harvard Guide to Contemporary American Writing*. Ed. Daniel Hoffman. Cambridge: Harvard UP, 1979. Print.

Smyth, Edmund J., ed. *Postmodernism and Contemporary Fiction*. London: Batsford, 1991. Print.

Thomas, Rhea. "The Metaphysics of Fear in Saul Bellow's *Henderson the Rain King*." *Saul Bellow Journal* 22.1 (2006): 35-46. Print.

Waugh, Patricia. 1984. *Metafiction: The Theory and Practice of Self-Conscious Fiction*. London: Methuen, 1984. Print.

Zarate, Tara Houligan. "'I Want, I Want!': Transcendental Epiphanies in Saul Bellow's *Henderson the Rain King*." *Saul Bellow Journal* 20.2 (Fall 2004): 41-50. Print.

Rewriting the Story, Restorying the Self
Doris Lessing's Experiments in Life-Writing

ÁNGELES DE LA CONCHA

Few writers have made wider use of their own life as fodder for their fiction than Doris Lessing. She is the author of a substantial autobiography in two volumes, *Under My Skin* (1994) and *Walking in the Shade* (1998), and of pieces of memoirs such as those gathered in *A Small Personal Voice*, and in the volume *Alfred and Emily* in which they stand side by side with a fictional biography of her parents. She has also written distinctly autobiographical novels such as the five volume series *The Children of Violence*,[1] as well as others with features either overtly autobiographical, as in *The Golden Notebook*, or more elliptical, as in *The Memoirs of a Survivor*, not to speak of the autobiographical elements the author herself has pointed at in other pieces of fiction, as is the case in *The Diary of a Good Neighbour* later published together with the sequel *If the Old Could* in the volume *The Diaries of Jane Somers*. An examination of the complex and fascinating relationship between her autobiography and her autobiographical fiction exceeds the scope of this paper.[2] Therefore, taking my cue from Paul Ricoeur, I shall focus my analysis of Lessing's life-writing on her fictional narratives considering, as Ricoeur does, that "by narrating a life of which" the actual writer "is not the author as to

---

1   The five volumes of *The Children of Violence* series will be hereafter referred to as *MQ* (*Martha Quest*), *PM* (*A Proper Marriage*), *RS* (*A Ripple from the Storm*), *LL* (*Landlocked*), and *FGC* (*The Four-Gated City*).
2   See De la Concha.

existence," she – Lessing – makes herself the "author as to its meaning." Moreover, since, as he argues, "due to the elusive character of real life we need the help of fiction to organize life retrospectively, after the fact, prepared to take as provisional and open to revision any figure of emplotment borrowed from fiction or from history" (*Oneself as Another* 162).

My reason for choosing Lessing's autobiographical fiction over her autobiography to dwell on her life-writing experiments is the privileged space literature opens for exploring in depth, first, the strenuous process of the constitution of the self, and second, the complex ethical issues involved at every step. As regards the former, Ricoeur interestingly comments how "in many narratives the self seeks its identity on the scale of an entire life" while, as regards the latter, he considers literature "a vast laboratory in which we experiment with estimations, evaluations, and judgments of approval and condemnation through which narrativity serves as a propaedeutic to ethics" (115). Lessing's autobiographical novels lend themselves particularly well to exploring the subjects of life-writing and the construction of narrative identity since they cover the span of the author's whole life, from *Martha Quest*, the first of the five volume series *Children of Violence*, published in 1952 when Lessing was thirty-three years old, to *The Sweetest Dream*, published in 2001, the year she turned eighty-three. The latter appeared when the third volume of her autobiography was expected and covered the period from the sixties to the eighties the volume was due to explore. However, as Lessing herself explains in the Author's Note that prefaces *The Sweetest Dream*, she chose the more fictive form so as not to hurt vulnerable people. She reasons that she has not "novelised autobiography" and "there are no parallels to actual people" but that her aim has been "to capture the spirit of the times." Yet it must be remembered that for Lessing the personal is inescapably related to the collective, and that she strongly believes in the role of the artist as interpreter of and witness to his/her time. In this sense, *The Sweetest Dream* can be considered a strikingly original form of life-writing, partaking of both fact and fiction and, most importantly, in discursive continuum with her previous autobiographical works. Indeed, strictly speaking, Lessing does not resume her autobiography proper, she retakes *The Four-Gated City*, the last volume of the fully acknowledged autobiographical series

Children of Violence, rewriting as it were a new version of her alter ego's – Martha Quest – later life, now from the vantage point of her own old age.

As in the series, the blending of fact and fiction is there, more factual at the level of discourse and historical events than at that of actual characters, though the protagonist, Frances, and her ex-husband Johnny Lennox, are reworks of Martha Quest and her second husband Anton Hesse, as both were, in turn, of Doris Lessing herself and her second husband Gottfried Anton Lessing. This life-writing process is perfectly in keeping with Ricoeur's belief, mentioned above, that we must organise life retrospectively with the help of fiction. Also, it fits in smoothly with the notion of interpretation as a way of self-understanding, as well as with the inescapable connection of narrative and time. Contrary to its obstinate association with decline, old age becomes in this sense a privileged standpoint to revisit one's life and refigure it providing an insightful comprehension of the positive, transformative temporal dimension of the self. Besides avoiding the risk of reducing identity to a single story, refiguring or "restorying" one's life may bring healing closure to troubling events, as Amelia DeFalco persuasively argues ("'And then–'" 78). In this regard, *The Sweetest Dream*, without evading events as painful as those Martha Quest has to face in *The Four-Gated City* both in the personal and the political realms, closes in a restorative mood, very different from the apocalyptic ending of the latter.

Both novels play with the duplicitous nature of dreams. The dream of idyllic order, harmony, and joy in *The City in the Desert* – the novel Mark Coldrige writes in *The Four-Gated City* – stands in utopian opposition to the double-faced London of the late fifties and sixties, where streets "of fashionable bright buildings" had behind them "avenues of nightmare squalor" *(FGC* 277), and in dystopian foreshadowing of the actual novel's ending with a whole civilization destroyed and people living on the edge in "deserts that once held gardens and *cities*" (611; emphasis added). The "sweet dreams" that punctuate and give name to Lessing's last experiment in autobiographical fiction expose the heavy toll deceitful political abstractions take on concrete individuals. But this time they also point at the actual possibility of achieving the happiness and the "good life" Ricoeur defines as "the nebulous of ideals and *dreams* of achievement with regard to which a life is held to be more or less fulfilled or unfulfilled" (*Oneself as Another* 179; emphasis added).

The fact that *The Sweetest Dreams* somehow retakes and crowns both Lessing's autobiography and her autobiographical novels makes more relevant its analysis from the vantage point of the author's old age. In the context of Lessing's life-writing, the novel, a condensed version of *Children of Violence* with a focus on *The Four-Gated City,* provides a panoramic view of the successful if strenuous building of narrative identity along the lines of an identity constructed through the dialectics of selfhood and otherness. For Ricoeur, the construction of identity requires a successful integration of the sense of the two words Latin has for the concept: *ipse*, in the sense of "oneself as self-same," and *idem*, in the sense of "being the same," the combination entailing qualities of a fundamental ethical nature, such as "self-constancy," loyalty, and openness to and responsibility for the other. These two attributes of identity are the elements of character, which is comprised of two dispositions. The first is habit, which once acquired, becomes "a distinctive sign by which a person is recognized"; the second, and most important, is "the set of *acquired identifications* by which the other enters into the composition of the same" (*Oneself as Another* 121). As Ricoeur argues:

> To a large extent, in fact, the identity of a person or a community is made up of these identifications with values, norms, ideals, models, and heroes, *in* which the person or the community recognizes itself. Recognizing oneself *in* contributes to recognizing oneself *by*. The identifications with heroic figures clearly display this otherness assumed as one's own, but this is already latent in the identification with values which make us place a cause above our own survival. An element of loyalty is thus incorporated into character and makes it turn toward fidelity, hence toward maintaining the self. Here the two poles of identity accord with one another. (121)

This process by which the other enters into the composition of the self is the crux of the matter in the development of the narrative identity of Lessing's alter ego heroine Martha Quest. It takes her a whole life – covered along five volumes – to find out the right values and ideals with which to identify. Too often, a lifetime is not enough for the task, particularly if, as in her case, it spans two World Wars followed by the Cold War and the threat of nuclear warfare. That is why Lessing will go on reworking unresolved issues until her own old age, from the perspective of which she will be able to heal the wounds she had dragged along since childhood.

Though born in 1919, the First World War would be a heavy and constant presence in Lessing's life through the indelible scars it left on both her parents. Her father was crippled in the war; her mother nursed him and later married him but theirs was not a romantic story. Her father, probably affected by shellshock, was uncommunicative and chronically ill. Her mother, resourceful, energetic, and highly sociable, found herself stifled in what turned to be an unproductive and rather desolate farm in the middle of British colonial Africa. In the foreword to *Alfred and Emily*, the fictional biography Lessing wrote about them when she had already turned eighty-nine imagining the life they might have lived had the Great War not happened, she starkly records:

> Shrapnel shattered my father's leg, and thereafter he had to wear a wooden one. He never recovered from the trenches. He died at sixty-two, an old man. On the death certificate it should have been written, as cause of death, the Great War. My mother's great love, a doctor, drowned in the Channel. She did not recover from that loss [...] That war, the Great War, the war that would end all war, squatted over my childhood. The trenches were as present to me as anything I actually saw around me. And here I still am, trying to get out from under that monstrous legacy, trying to get free. (1)

In her essay "The Small Personal Voice" Lessing claims ethical judgment as the responsibility of the artist to provide "illumination in order to enlarge one's perception of life" (9), and describes the theme of her series of novels *The Children of Violence* as "a study of the individual conscience in its relations with the collective" (18), an idea she expands in the Preface to the second edition of *The Golden Notebook*. There she argues that, for the artist, "nothing is personal in the sense that is uniquely one's own [...]. Writing about oneself, one is writing about others, since your problems, pains, pleasures, emotions – and your extraordinary and remarkable ideas – can't be yours alone" (13). This allows her, as Gayle Greene puts it, to "see herself as child and heir to the war" and "to make 'children of violence' her metaphor for all of us living in the twentieth century, all of us begotten, born, and bred in the aftermath or preparation for war" (2). Lessing's awareness of the illuminating nature of literature and of the artist as seer is in line with the Romantic vision of poetry as a means of improving the human condition and of the poet's deep empathy with the rest of humanity. It is also in line with Ricoeur's more rigorous philosophical analysis of the ethical implications of narrative, particularly as regards the question of narrative identity, that is, the role narrative plays in the constitution of the self. As Karl Simms explains, "we understand our own lives – our own selves and our own places in the world – by interpreting our lives as if they were narratives, or, more precisely, through the work of interpreting our lives we turn them into narratives, and life understood as narrative constitutes self-understanding" (80).

In Lessing's life-writing war and parenthood, inextricably entwined, loom large. In *Under My Skin,* the first volume of her autobiography, she recalls her mother "telling [her] over and over again that she had not wanted a girl, she wanted a boy" (25). The lack of maternal love pursued her all throughout her life: "I knew from the beginning she did not love me [...]. My early childhood made me one of the walking wounded for years," she goes on to say (25). This biographical statement will be fleshed out throughout Lessing's life-writing. Her mother's lack of affection and constant nagging deeply affect the process of identity formation of Martha Quest, thwarting the mother-daughter bond and thereby preventing the daughter's first fundamental identification with her mother. Feeling unloved, Martha becomes a rebellious difficult girl fighting her mother at every turn, their relationship becoming increasingly strained as she grows up. "My memories of my mother are all of antagonism and fighting," she writes in the autobiographical piece "Impertinent Daughters" (113). Her mother personifies the features of womanhood she will come to detest, maternity above all but also the petty small-mindedness of the colonial provincial town, its classism and racism. Martha will relentlessly retaliate with the weapons at hand, sexuality at first, somewhat naively making a point of not only being "attractive sexually, but good in bed" because of her mother's "rooted dislike for all matters sexual" (*PM* 309); then, marriage, literature, politics, and finally, leaving Africa to live in London. When failing to identify herself with her mother or any other female figure, Martha turns to literature for heroines on whom to model herself only to realise that the alternatives books provide are insipid feminine creatures, untruthful useless creations (229), cultural myths responding to "what men, or the men-women, wished they were" (73). Refusing to give up her ideals of a "good life" she refashions an old dream she had when she was barely an adolescent girl of a large welcoming house in which white and black and brown adults and children happily mixed together (*MQ* 21), now including herself as the character she would like to become:

Since there was no woman she had ever met she could *model* herself on, she created a brooding and female spirit in that large cool house in the avenues. Six or seven children, not just two – a brood, then, of children who fed from this source of warmth and creativeness as at a spring […]. One of those warm, large, delightful maternal humorous females she would be, undemanding, unpossessive. One never met them, but if she put her mind to it, no doubt she could be one. (*PM* 303; emphasis added)

Marriage, which had become the means to escape the constriction of her family life, a microcosm of the colonial world outside, soon proves she had broken out of one cage to enter another in which she was just as firmly entrapped. Greene points out the clusters of metaphors that are conspicuously suggesting the snares of a femininity she has internalised as the only model available and which she struggles to break from: "the cycles of procreation" and "birth" and "the circles of friends and women which work together with imagery of nets, webs, cages, bonds, traps" (44). Eventually, Martha comes to see that it is not just her biological mother but "Nature, that great mother" (*PM* 174) that locks women in making of them "pawns in the hands of an old fatality" (109):

She saw her mother […] confronting her Victorian father, the patriarchal father, with rebellion. She saw herself sitting where her mother now sat, a woman horribly metamorphosed, entirely dependent on her children for any interest in life, resented by them and resenting them […]. This nightmare of a class and generation: repetition. (109)

The nightmare becomes all too real when she finds herself actually repeating with her baby daughter her mother's pattern of feeling and behaviour. She senses she deeply dislikes the child in the context of swollen breasts and disgust at milk flowing (172), accepts that her daughter bores her to exhaustion (227, 229), that not only does she not miss her but can even hate her (176) and is utterly unable to enjoy her (224), until in a tumult of misery and guilt "she ha[s] the honesty to admit that she was as unfit for maternity as her mother" (227). At this point Martha makes up her mind to break out of that unbearable nightmare by setting her daughter free from what she sees as the vicious circle of the mother-daughter dyad.

The series *The Children of Violence* makes clear the indelible life-long consequences of the impossibility of establishing sound identifications, with the mother to begin with, of which the first and foremost is the inability to mother. In this regard, Lessing seems to make a point of connecting the personal with the collective. It is significant that both Martha's daughter and mother are named after Lessing's own paternal grandmother whose first and second names – Caroline and May – they respectively carry. May is Doris Lessing's second name, which seems to underline the unity of life-writing, fact and fiction springing from the same emotional source, and to hint at the harmful nature of the biological chain in a strongly patriarchal society, of which the British colony was the paradigm. By the end of *A Proper Marriage*, Martha, albeit "appalled at her own cruelty," has broken away both from her mother, whose mere touch she finds "unpleasant" (288), and her baby daughter for whom she has to admit she feels no love, "nothing but the bond of responsibility" (294).

For Ricoeur, responsibility, or the commitment to respond to the other's need, requires reciprocity and self-constancy, the essentially ethical qualities of the two poles of identity, when *ipse* and *idem* coincide in the concept of narrative identity. As he argues,

Self-constancy is for each person that manner of conducting himself or herself so that other can count on that person. Because someone is counting on me, I am accountable for my actions before another. The term "responsibility" unites both meanings "counting on" and "being accountable for." It unites them, adding to them the idea of a response to the question "Where are you"? asked by another who needs me. This response is the following: "Here I am!" a response that is a statement of self-constancy. (*Oneself as Another* 165)

Obviously, the person who needs me can count on me only if I am there to respond "Here I am." Martha's promise of freedom to her small daughter unilaterally cutting her off for good without regard for the unbridgeable dissymmetry of their positions is not just a "silly wager," as Ricoeur calls "a commitment that [does] not involve doing something that the other could choose or prefer" (267), but an act of profound violence that far from responding to the child's need turns her into a radical other and bars them both from entering into the composition of their respective selves. Martha thus becomes one of the troubling cases of selfhood deprived of, or lacking, the support of sameness, that is, the pole of identity which is formed out of the acquired identifications with others.

Along the three following volumes of the series, having broken free from family ties and friends, from the suffocating provincial colonial atmosphere and its pervading sexism, racism, and classism, Martha looks elsewhere for those values and models that may help her fulfil her ideals and find the "good life" she recurrently dreams of. In *A Ripple in the Storm* she turns to politics becoming an active member of the Communist party and eventually marries a fellow Communist, German-born Anton Hesse, her group's leader. Yet she soon realises the difficulty of change, since the party and group politics, underneath the apparent radicalism of their anti-establishment posturing, are permeated by the same sexism, racism, and will to power she had known so well before, undercutting the ideals they proclaimed daily. Despite Martha's initial exhilaration at her new life, at the ideal of a better world promised by a true revolution of the people, she finds herself caught again in the traps of marriage and of the same sexual politics she had attempted to escape, her predicament worsened by the disappointment at realizing the impossible distance between political abstractions and people's everyday life, hers included. Claire Sprague interestingly notes the "signs of Martha's acute dissatisfaction with herself and her need for a *model*" (137; emphasis added) that she tries to assuage in a deep and total loyalty to the political group which quickly replaces her family in her affections and full commitment. "The group is mother, father, sister, brother, children" (138), Sprague states, while observing the same process of disillusion setting in that causes Martha to be "more divided than ever and in the narrowest cage she has ever known" (132).

A Ripple in the Storm ends with only three people left from the initial communist group and the dispiriting image of Martha laying down in bed, her back to her second husband, Anton, "sliding into sleep like a diver weighted with lead" (262). *Landlocked*, with her second divorce, the group dissolved, political illusions crashed and Martha encircled by the same awful ring of rage, impotence, and guilt she had tried to break out of realizing "[s]he could no more dissociate herself from the violence done her, done by her, than a tadpole can live out of water" (202). Images of warfare, fighters, chaos and cities in ruins all over Europe (43, 57, 58, 121) merge with personal, marital, and family strife and with her own pressing need to move out of the circle metaphorically represented by the key-ring with the half-century-old black, rusty keys her mother presents her with on learning she is going to England. By the end of the novel, she feels the weight of the two wars on her soul, making of her "the essence of violence," having "been conceived, bred, fed and reared on violence" (202). Seething with anger and impotence over her mother's insistence on her meeting the child she had left, still looking in vain for models in literature aware that there were no precedents for the unnaturalness "of leaving a child without the wailing, the weeping, the wringing of hands that [would] make it almost an act within nature" in novels, dramas or poems she could remember (238-39), and profoundly disappointed in politics, she sees no other way to escape than by leaving the African continent and her whole life behind.

The Four-Gated City opens with Martha's arrival in post-war London, a "dull brown grey city," "all cracked and thinned and darkened by war" (35) in whose anonymity she delights at first enjoying the perfect freedom of a free floating identity. "What difference did it make to her, the sense of identity, like a silent statement '*I am here*'?" she thinks for a while, until she feels she must "become responsible for her fellow beings," and realises, if only out of a sense of self-preservation, the importance of being able to give one's name to the person who asks "What is your name? Who are you?" (17; emphasis added). These question marks are at the core of the last volume of the series. Martha soon feels that her old self has vanished, that "*she* was nothing to do with Martha or any other name she might have had attached to her, nothing to do with what she looked like, how she had been shaped" (36). She thinks of her little daughter Caroline and she finds it hard "to tell, whether she was Martha, or her mother who had given birth to her, or Caroline who would give birth" (55).

In *Dreams and Nightmares* Ernest Hartmann explores the importance of dreams in the task of self-understanding and as facilitators of the development and restoration of the self, particularly after trauma. "Dreams are guided by the dominant emotion or concern of the dreamer," he argues (61, 117). They function as explanatory metaphors by "making connections more broadly than waking [...] bringing together subnets in the mind, finding overlaps between patterns, and thus noting and picturing similarities" (117). The confusion of herself, her mother, and her daughter without being able to discern who gave birth to whom, all three undistinguishable in the startling image, points to the trauma at the source of Martha's fundamental lack of maternal love and her subsequent inability to mother. The same lack Lessing acknowledged she herself had suffered (*Under My Skin* 25). Children in a similar predicament haunt Martha in nightmares in *The Four-Gated City*. In one she dreams she is in a house in London full of children and half-grown people with "faces tortured and hurt," with her as "a middle-aged woman with an anxious face, a face set to endure" (59-60). In another she finds herself in yet another London house again with sad half-grown children, responsible for them, once more "worried" and "anxious." But this time "she held the fort, she manned defences" (71). In the second dream the progress is noticeable since she sees herself responding and there is a hint of hope that she may succeed in "being there," that is, be receptive to the appeal from the other in the sense Ricoeur explores in *Oneself as Another*.

The visions are premonitory, foreshadowing the path she will take by accepting the first job she is offered as secretary to a writer, Mark Coldridge, agreeing to take care of his son while his wife is undergoing psychiatric treatment. The lodging taken as a temporary arrangement until she finds something more suitable eventually becomes the large house of her recurring dreams, set in the real hard post-war world, herself at the centre responsible for holding the house together and for an assorted group of half-grown-up children as damaged by the indelible traces the Second World War has left on their parents as she herself had been by those the First had left on hers. This makes her particularly sensitive to their plight as well as to that of their either neurotic, depressed, or mentally deranged mothers, able to understand them and respond to their needs.

Gayle Greene points at the mixed critical reception *The Four-Gated City* has met, from impatience at the seemingly repetitious circles Martha allows herself to enter, her passivity and procrastination, her willing circumscription to the boundaries of surrogate wife and mother when she had twice shed marriage and shunned family life, and her voluntary confinement to the realm of femininity after her determination to escape it, all of which have made readers wonder why she couldn't do something more original (75). However, this criticism ignores that both Martha's mood and the nature of her experience are utterly different. Alone and anonymous in London, she looks back on her life and realises she hardly knew herself. She is unable to recognise the Martha of the past and feels she has to rebuild her identity from scratch. At the brink of dissolution, immensely tired to the point of thinking of death and suicide (*FGC* 191), she turns inwards painstakingly "wrest[ling] herself out of the dark and enter[ing] places in herself she had not known were there" (286). Yet it would be wrong to infer that the narrative shifts its focus to the realm of the personal. As mentioned above, Lessing had explicitly defined the theme of the series *The Children of Violence* as "a study of the individual conscience in its relations with the collective" ("The Small Personal Voice" 18). In this last volume of the series Martha clearly stands in a metonymic relationship with the collective, as the house and its inhabitants do with the post-war world outside. Martha sees herself as "a mass of fragments, or facets, or bits of mirror" (*FGC* 336) in the centre of a house in which "all was a mass of small separate things, surfaces, shapes, all needing different attention, different kinds of repair" (336), while feeling that "this was the real truth of what went on not only here but everywhere: everything declined and frayed and came to pieces in one's hands [...] a mass of fragments, like a smashed mirror" (337).

For Ricoeur, the most dramatic transformations of personal identity pass through the trial of the shattering or the nothingness of identity. This "imagined nothingness of the self becomes the existential 'crisis' of the self" (*Oneself as Another* 166), and the only way out is "the ethical primacy of the other [rather] than the self over the self" (168). "The ego 'encumbered' by the self, the ego before its encounter with the other is a stubbornly closed, locked up, separate ego," he says (337) following Levinas albeit departing from him in his privileging regard for the others out of solicitude rather than duty. It is in its opening to the other, by allowing the other to enter into the composition of the same, that the self is able to reach the aim of an accomplished life, in the ethical terms mentioned above of "*'the good life' with and for others, in just institutions*" (172).

In *The Four-Gated City* we follow Martha as she struggles to achieve this aim. She reconstructs her identity slowly and carefully, aware "that the Martha she had created during the last few years was fragile, and might easily again be lost into the dark" (286). She does so by becoming an observer and identifying her old self with the difficult youngsters now in her care: "Every time Martha wished she could slap Gwen or tell Jill that she was a monster – she remembered Martha Quest" (369). "I was like this, I did that, I felt that and this: Francis, Paul, Jill and the rest, they were me, I was what they are" (428), she thinks, grateful to them in the end for the opportunity they offer her "to pay off debts" (431). It is because she understands them that she is able to feel that sympathy for the suffering other that arises from "the shared admission of fragility" (Ricoeur, *Oneself as Another* 192). Martha is ruefully aware of the fate that awaited them, very similar to her own, as children of violent times growing up in the dysfunctional institutions of marriage and families shattered by war, in a materialist society in the hands of corrupted strife-ridden political parties, self-serving governments, and multinational corporations.

The Four-Gated City is a long dense novel, roughly spanning two decades, from the late forties to the late sixties, plus an Appendix which looks back on the following two decades from a date close to the end of the century. The personal and the political are closely interweaved and, as we follow Martha's change in her quest for her true self and "the good life" she had dreamed of, we witness in parallel "the whirlwind of change" (*The Small Personal Voice* 15) blowing all over the West, with London and the Coldriges' house as its paradigmatic centre. Lessing seems to believe that a civilization ravaged by violence cannot truly change for the better but is doomed to destruction. In keeping with the connection between the individual and the collective, the volume closes with the house of Martha's dreams on the verge of being pulled down and the family dispersed. An Appendix follows with reports of what looks like the desolate aftermath of a Third World War that has brought about the collapse of the West and Martha's own death, communicated in a brief note, which suggests the impossibility of a full reconstitution of the self after a deeply traumatic experience.

In reality, despite Martha's commitment to paying off her debts – "her little daughter Caroline, the two men she had married so absurdly – her mother" (*FGC* 38) – she does not really accomplish the task. She manages to solve the problem only vicariously, by entering into a peculiar *ménage a trois* with Mark Coldrige and his mentally deranged wife Lynda, which suits all three of them in striking subversion of *Jane Eyre*'s impossible marriage triangle, and by caring for their son and the assorted ill-adapted psychologically wounded youths gathered in their large house. But her little daughter Caroline is banished from her mind for good and Martha is unable to make peace with her mother when Mrs. Quest comes to London for a visit. Martha has a nervous breakdown and they part never to see each other again.

The *Children of Violence* series was written along a timespan of almost twenty years. The first volume was published in 1952, when Lessing was thirty-three and the last in 1969 when she had turned fifty. It would take her another fourteen years to really "pay off" her "debts" as regards her child and her mother. In 1974 *The Memoirs of a Survivor* was released, although it was written five years before when Lessing was fifty-five, and in 1982, having turned sixty-three, Lessing published pseudonymously *The Diary of a Good Neighbour*, which was republished one year later with its sequel *If the Old Could* in one volume entitled *The Diaries of Jane Somers*.

It was Lessing herself that called attention to the autobiographical substance of both novels, a fact that had been overlooked by critics, and which points at the nature of life-writing, freely partaking of both fact and fiction. *The Memoirs of a Survivor* weaves together the disturbing vision Martha had of herself, her baby, and her mother at the beginning of *The Four-Gated City*, and the cataclysmic scenery of the Appendix that closes it. The novel opens in an unnamed dystopian city on the verge of collapse, overrun by gangs, its inhabitants awaiting evacuation. The protagonists are a woman of whom we know little else than that she lives in a house one of whose walls surreally opens into a labyrinthine mansion in ruins and a young girl inexplicably entrusted to her in the midst of the chaotic besieged city. The novel breaks with all the rules of realism, the action taking place in two oneiric spaces, the inner realm of dreams and the outer world of the nightmarish dystopian streets. However, soon we realise that the scenes and the characters in the mansion the unnamed woman enters behind the wall ring a familiar bell. To begin with, the name of the young protagonist in the outer world and of the little girl in the scenes in the inner one is Emily, the first name of both Doris Lessing's mother and maternal grandmother. The scenes in the inner world picturing the unloved little girl blamed by her mother who prefers her baby brother are also familiar, as well as the merging of all the female figures, the little girl, the mother, and the mother's mother, together with that of the narrator, at times undistinguishable from the child. The ending, though, is totally different from that of *The Four-Gated City*. The unnamed protagonist is able to make peace with the little girl her mother had been, with her own little daughter, and with the girl she herself was, the surrealist genre allowing for a visionary "breakthrough to another world and way of knowing" which "does not require the breakdown of the individual," as happened to Martha but is in keeping with the reconciliation and fantasy that characterise the closure of Shakespeare's romances (Greene 157).

In a similar vein, though in the radically different genre of down-to-earth realism, in *The Diary of a Good Neighbour* Lessing sets out to make her peace with the rather more formidable figure of the mother. As in the case of *The Memoirs of a Survivor*, it was Lessing herself who pointed out the biographical nature of the novel, specifically associating the character traits of the two main fictional characters with her own mother. Interestingly, she gives the milder, more positive and attractive features of her mother to the protagonist, Jane Somers, leaving the more difficult traits to Maudie, the old woman Jane befriends and cares for, coming to genuinely love her. In actual fact, Jane Somers is probably closer to the daughter Lessing herself would have liked to become and Maudie to the woman her mother, whose second name was also Maude, would have become had she reached the same old age. As Greene perceptively sums up, "one function of the Jane Somers pseudonym was to allow Lessing to deal with matters she could not confront as Doris Lessing, still cathected matters related to the mother" (190).

In *Memory, History, Forgetting*, Ricoeur turns to Freud's essay "Remembering, Repeating and Working-Through" to stress the processes necessary to reconcile the patient with repressed material in order to achieve forgiveness (70). Memories of their old selves haunt the protagonists of these novels, all alter-egos of Lessing, some also of Martha Quest, in narratives abounding in patterns of replaying and repetition through which they "restory" their selves. To remember we also need others that provide us with access to events reconstructed for us from a different viewpoint (*Memory, History, Forgetting* 121). In *The Diary of a Good Neighbour* Jane's niece bluntly reminds her of her unkindness to her mother which, to her, explains the unusual relationship Jane engages in with the destitute old woman. As Greene puts it, "the protagonist enters into a surrogate mother-daughter relationship in order to atone for failures with her biological mother" (194). What is interesting is that from her self-encapsulated ego, Jane moves to a new sense of identity constructed in relation to another, "accepting the responsibility and adhering to the *'promise'* it entails" (Greene 194; emphasis added).

At this stage, Lessing was fully prepared to retake Martha's story and provide a new version. The reconciliation in *The Memoirs of a Survivor* with the child she was and her mother had been, together with the response she is able to give to the young girl entrusted to her – as opposed to the spurious promise made to her baby daughter in *A Proper Marriage* –, and with her biological mother through Maudie Fowler in *The Diary of a Good Neighbour*, allow the author a new perspective from which to rewrite *The Four-Gated City*. She would do so in *The Sweetest Dream*, published in 2001 when she had turned eighty-two and thirty-two years after the publication of *The Four-Gated City*. For Ricoeur, the narrative unity of a life, "which may be seen as an unstable mixture of fabulation and actual experience" (*Oneself as Another* 162), is governed "by a life project, however uncertain and mobile it may be, and by fragmentary practices which have their own unity" (158). The mixture of fabulation and experience is at the basis of the novels we have seen, all of them governed by their female protagonist's project of a "good life" envisioned in dreams in which she herself featured as "a warm, maternal, undemanding, unpossessive, humorous female" (*PM* 303) in the midst of a brood of children entrusted to her care. In her essay "The Small Personal Voice" Lessing claimed that because of the "dangerous, violent, explosive and precarious" nature of the times after the discovery of the atom bomb, "the great dream and the great nightmare of centuries of human thought have taken flesh and walk beside us all, day and night." Since "artists are the traditional interpreters of dreams and nightmares," she argued, "this is no time to turn our backs on our chosen responsibilities, which is what we would be doing if we refused to share in the deep anxieties, terrors and hopes of human beings everywhere" (11).

As mentioned above, the title *The Sweetest Dream* refers both to dreams and nightmares. As opposed to the predominantly nightmarish quality of Martha's dreams in *The Four-Gated City* foreshadowing the narrative's apocalyptical ending, in *The Sweetest Dream*, Frances Lennox – the protagonist, who is clearly Martha Quest's alter-ego – finally attains that "good life" whose content, as already stated, is that "nebulous of ideals and dreams of achievement with regard to which a life is held to be more or less fulfilled or unfulfilled" (Ricoeur, *Oneself as Another* 179). Though reworking motifs and characters of the four first volumes of the *Children of Violence* series, particularly the couple Martha and Anton, *The Sweetest Dream* is a distinct rewriting of the fifth, *The Four-Gated City*. Both novels share a similar setting and characters: a London house, full of assorted half-grown mostly difficult children entrusted to the protagonist's care, in both cases a middle-aged woman, ex-wife of a political activist forgetful of family responsibilities. Both households accommodate depressive ex-wives lodged in the basement. Both households stand in metonymic relationship with their respective times sharing in their "anxieties, terrors and hopes" ("The Small Personal Voice" 11) by being witness to and exposing the political events and the social phenomena whose effects leave their mark on the children who still bear the traces of war. Despite the different time covered by both novels, in *The Sweetest Dream* the youngsters are still damaged creatures. Julia, Frances's mother in law, says they are "children of war, not normal" (138). "What right have we to expect any sort of normality? With the history of our family? All war and disruption and the comrades?" (339) – drunkenly confirms Colin, Frances' son.

The Sweetest Dreams pointedly alludes to the false dreams of liberation of the politicians' promises (401, 419, 477-478) particularly exemplified in "the windy rhetoric" (226) of dazzling Comrade Johnny Lennox, Frances's ex-husband, who embodies Ricoeur's description of the unjust man, the one "who takes too much in terms of advantages […] or not enough in terms of burdens" (*Oneself as Another* 201). But there are also the good dreams that come true breaking the nightmarish chains that had so imprisoned Martha and from which Frances is able to set herself free by learning to say, "yes, yes, to what was happening, and consciously saying it, accepting what had arrived in front of her, as was now her philosophy" (*SD* 68).

One of the striking differences between Frances and Martha results from Lessing's resolution of the mother-daughter conflict that had weighed so heavily on Martha – and on Lessing herself – throughout their lives. Despite the similitude of their weariness at the responsibilities they are landed with and learn to accept out of solicitude for the vulnerable other, Martha is caught in the circle of guilt, resentment, and reparation, of "paying debts," while in Frances's case solicitude "unfolds the dialogic dimension of self-esteem," which to Ricoeur (*Oneself as Another* 180) provides the stability upon which friendship, based on reciprocity and equality, rests. This concept of solicitude is more inclusive since it joins its ethical aim with the ethics of affect. Ricoeur summarises it as

the range of attitudes deployed between the two extremes of the summons to responsibility, where the initiative comes from the other, and of sympathy for the suffering other, where the initiative comes from the loving self, friendship appearing as a midpoint where the self and the other share equally the same wish to live together. (192)

At eighty-three, Lessing's narrative powers are intact and, significantly, allow her to look back on her life-writing and rewrite it from a perspective that not only provides an increased ethical understanding but offers an alternative to what DeFalco describes as the "oppressively grim cultural scripts of ageing" (*Uncanny Subjects* 128), boldly challenging cultural clichés that pronounce happiness and marriage based on friendship and love in old age impossible. As such, we see Frances into her seventies, with a busy professional life, happily married to an old good friend, a journalist ten years younger than her. In the lively communal house of Martha's dreams, having brought up alone her two sons and a brood of ill-adapted children, and cared for all sorts of neurotic mothers, she feels "as if she had stumbled so late in her life, as in a fairy tale, into a glade full of sunshine" (*SD* 337):

Frances would wake from a dream and tell herself, and then Rupert, that she had been dreaming of happiness. Let them mock who would, and they certainly did, but there was such a thing as happiness and here it was, here they were, both of them, contented, like cats in the sun. But these two middle-aged people – courtesy would call them that – cuddled to themselves a secret they knew would shrivel if exposed. And they were not the only ones: ideology has pronounced their condition impossible and so, people keep quiet. (338)

Frances's indulging in happy dreams, which have come true, defies the cultural view of ageing as a narrative of inevitable decline (Gullette 2004). The happy ending, on the other hand, does not in the least imply a refuge from the world outside since the personal and the collective are joined as ever in Lessing's work. Through the lives of the children Frances has brought up and cared for, Lessing gives an accurate portrait of the conflicts of the time at home moving on to focus on those of postcolonial Southern Rhodesia, today Zimbabwe. There, Lessing, through her alter-ego Martha Quest, had started her life journey in a *quest* for the self to find it in London, fifty years later, through Frances Lennox, Martha's second self. All in all, it will take Lessing a whole life and several re-stories to construct a narrative identity whose growth discloses the fascinating albeit arduous process of the constitution of an ethical identity through the dialectic relation of selfhood and otherness.

REFERENCES

De la Concha, Ángeles. "Autobiografía y ficción: discursos en competencia en la obra de Doris Lessing." *Cartografías del yo*. Ed. Julia Salmerón and Ana I. Zamorano. Madrid: Instituto de Investigaciones Feministas and Editorial Complutense, 2006. 313-40. Print.

DeFalco, Amelia. *Uncanny Subjects. Aging in Contemporary Narrative*. Columbus: Ohio State UP, 2010. Print.

---. "'And then–': Narrative Identity and Uncanny Aging in *The Stone Angel*." *Canadian Literature* 198 (Autumn 2008): 75-89. Print.

Greene, Gayle. *Doris Lessing. The Poetics of Change*. Ann Arbor: U of Michigan P, 1994. Print.

Gullette, Margaret M. *Aged by Culture*. Chicago: U of Chicago P, 2004.

Hartmann, Ernest. *Dreams and Nightmares. The Origin and Meaning of Dreams*. New York: Perseus, 2001. Print.

Lessing, Doris. *Alfred and Emily*. London: Harper, 2008. Print.

---. *The Sweetest Dream*. London: Flamingo, 2001. Print.

--- *Walking in the Shade: Volume Two of My Autobiography, 1949-1962*. London: Flamingo, 1999, Print.

---. "Impertinent Daughters." Doris Lessing. *A Small Personal Voice. Essays, Reviews, Interviews*. Ed. Paul Schlueter. London: Flamingo, 1994. 101-57. Print.

---. *A Small Personal Voice. Essays, Reviews, Interviews*. Ed. Paul Schlueter. London: Flamingo, 1994. Print.

---. "The Small Personal Voice." *A Small Personal Voice. Essays, Reviews, Interviews*. Ed. Paul Schlueter. London: Flamingo, 1994. 7-25. Print.

---. *Under My Skin. Volume One of My Autobiography, to 1949*. London: Harper, 1994. Print.
---. *The Golden Notebook*. 1962. London: Flamingo, 1993. Print.
---. *The Four-Gated City*. 1969. London: Penguin, 1991. Print.
---. *The Memoirs of a Survivor*. 1974. London: Vintage Books, 1988. Print.
---. *The Diaries of Jane Somers*. London: Vintage, 1984. Print.
---. *If the Old Could*. London: Michael Joseph, 1984. Print.
---. *Landlocked*. 1965. London: Granada, 1984. Print.
---. *The Diary of a Good Neighbour*. London: Michael Joseph, 1983. Print.
---. *A Proper Marriage*. 1954. London: Granada, 1981. Print.
---. *Martha Quest*. 1952. New York: New American Library, 1970. Print.
---. *A Ripple from the Storm*. 1958. London: Granada, 1970. Print.
Ricoeur, Paul. *Memory, History, Forgetting*. Chicago: U of Chicago P, 2006. Print.
---. *Oneself as Another*. Trans. Kathleen Blamey. Chicago: U of Chicago P, 1994. Print.
Simms, Karl. *Paul Ricoeur*. London: Routledge, 2003. Print.
Sprague, Claire. *Rereading Doris Lessing. Narrative Patterns of Doubling and Repetition*. Chapel Hill: U of North Carolina P, 1987. Print.

Contributors

Collado-Rodríguez, Francisco is Professor of American Literature at the University of Zaragoza (Spain). He has written extensively on the influence of fantasy, myth, trauma, and scientific discourse on recent American fiction. His articles have appeared in journals such as *Critique*, *Studies in the Novel*, *Papers on Language and Literature*, and *Journal of Modern Literature*. He has authored and edited a number of books, among them *Chuck Palahniuk* published by Bloomsbury in 2013.

De la Concha, Ángeles is Professor of English Studies at the UNED (Spain). She co-authored *English Literature in the Second Half of the 20th Century* (2006) and *Ejes de la literatura inglesa medieval y renacentista* (2010) and edited *Shakespeare en la imaginación contemporánea. Revisiones y reescrituras de su obra* (2004) and *El sustrato cultural de la violencia de género. Literatura, cine, arte y videojuegos* (2010). She has published numerous articles and book chapters on gender issues and feminist theory and on postmodern fiction.

Cerezo Moreno, Marta is Associate Professor of English at the UNED (Spain). Her main areas of interest and publications focus on contemporary English narrative in relation to Literary Gerontology and Disability Studies, and on Early Modern British Literature, especially Shakespearean drama. She has published articles on works by A. S. Byatt, John Updike, Margaret Atwood, John Banville, and Anne Tyler and also on Chaucer, Shakespeare, and the tragic hero on the Elizabethan stage. She has published two books about medieval and Renaissance literature and criticism. She is a member of the research project *New Critical Approaches to the Trace and the Application to Recent Literature in English* (FFI2013-44154-P).

Gibert, Teresa is Professor of English at the UNED (Spain). Her publications on American and Canadian literature include essays in the collections *T. S. Eliot at the Turn of the Century* (Lund UP), *T. S. Eliot and Our Turning World* (Macmillan), *Telling Stories: Postcolonial Short Fiction in English* (Rodopi), *Postcolonial Ghosts* (PUM), *Stories Through Theories / Theories Through Stories* (Michigan State UP), *The Cambridge History of Canadian Literature* (Cambridge UP), and *Short Story Theories: A Twenty-First-Century Perspective* (Rodopi).

Gravagne, Pamela teaches courses on ageing, gender, and film in both Women's Studies and American Studies at the University of New Mexico. She is the author of *The Becoming of Age: Cinematic Visions of Mind, Body and Identity in Later Life* (2013) and has published numerous articles on ageing, film, time, and memory. She is currently investigating the effects of post-colonial and post-human thought on the construction of narratives about ageing and old age.

MacDonald, Anna is a Research Associate at Monash University, Australia. She has a PhD in Literary Studies and has published on the writings of W. G. Sebald and Gaston Bachelard as well as in the field of contemporary art. Dr. MacDonald is currently engaged in a critical examination of W. G. Sebald's spatial poetics.

Miquel-Baldellou, Marta is a member of the research group Dedal-lit, affiliated with the English Department of the University of Lleida which specialises in cultural gerontology and ageing studies. Within the framework of the research project *Aging and Gender in Contemporary Literary Creation in English* (FFI2012-37050) – which the Dedal-Lit group was awarded with by the Ministry of Economy and Competitiveness in 2012 – she is looking into ageing in the late short fiction of the writer Daphne du Maurier. The results of her current research have been recently published in books such as *Myths in Crisis: The Crisis of Myth* (Cambridge Scholars Publishing) and *Literary Creativity and the Older Woman Writer: A Collection of Critical Essays* (Peter Lang).

Rivera Godoy-Benesch, Rahel is a researcher and lecturer at the University of Zurich, currently completing her PhD project on narrative portraits of ageing artists. In collaboration with Pro Senectute Switzerland, she has also conducted a study of a corpus of roughly 1,000 narratives of old age which has concluded in a book on literary gerontology (2015). Her research interests include theories of late style, creativity, and genre, as well as the intersection between literature, science, and society.

Pascual Soler, Nieves teaches American Literature at the University of Jaén. Her research interests cover cultural studies, feminism, food, and popular culture. She has co-edited: *Masculinities, Femininities and the Power of Hybrid in U.S. Narratives* (2007); *Feeling in Others* (2008); *Stories Through Stories, Theories Through Stories* (2009); and *Comidas bastardas* (2013). Her work has appeared in journals such as *Mosaic*, *Style*, *Journal of Intercultural Studies* and *Food, Culture and Society*. She is a member of the research project *New Critical Approaches to the Trace and the Application to Recent Literature in English* (FFI2013-44154-P).

Strauss, Sara is a postdoc at the University of Paderborn, Germany. Her research interests focus on narratology, neuroethics, and ageing studies. Her monograph *"This Bright Inward Cinema of Thought": Stream of Consciousness in Contemporary English Fiction* (Trier: WVT, 2013) centres on narrative approaches to the mind-body problem and related neuroethical issues. She is currently working on a project on the representation of old age and dementia in English-language literature and culture.